"WHAT'S YOUR FAVORITE SONG?"

The Life, Family and Music of
George and Emma Kelly

"WHAT'S YOUR FAVORITE SONG?"

*The Life, Family and Music of
George and Emma Kelly*

G. Ross Kelly

authorHOUSE®

AuthorHouse™
1663 Liberty Drive
Bloomington, IN 47403
www.authorhouse.com
Phone: 1 (800) 839-8640

Published by AuthorHouse 03/04/2015

ISBN: 978-1-4969-6957-6 (sc)
ISBN: 978-1-4969-6958-3 (hc)
ISBN: 978-1-4969-6956-9 (e)

Library of Congress Control Number: 2015902494

Print information available on the last page.

Any people depicted in stock imagery provided by Thinkstock are models,
and such images are being used for illustrative purposes only.
Certain stock imagery © *Thinkstock.*

This book is printed on acid-free paper.

Contents

Part 3-Growing Up

Part 4-Fame Comes Calling

Acknowledgements

This book was written with the help of many people, in particular my brothers and sisters, and my extended family. I will begin with my brothers and sisters:

Kitty Kelly Walters
Phoebe Kelly Collins
Jackie Kelly Hinz
Paula Kelly Rogers
Bill Kelly
Emaline Kelly Perdoni
Mike Kelly
Pete Kelly
Pat Kelly Alley

Each of them provided stories, context and perspective on the life we shared together as a family. Most of all, they provided their support and encouragement. Paula and Jackie were invaluable with their knowledge, time and resources to put together the many photographs that accompany this narrative and the historical accounting of the people, places and events that are referenced. Pat also provided many invaluable insights and stories from her unique perspective as the 'baby' of the Kelly family.

Additionally, my former wife, Brenda, was an equally invaluable resource, as she remains closely linked to my brothers and sisters and our entire family. Also, my sons, Brett and Rob, my daughter, Erin, and my many in-laws, nieces and nephews all contributed stories and context to this narrative.

G. Ross Kelly

I want to thank my friends who served as proof readers and advisors, especially Jennifer Parker, whose knowledge of my family, combined with her knowledge of the art of southern literature, helped to guide me through this entire project. My partners at _Emma_Said Productions were also invaluable to me in preparing this book, especially Ms. Brandi Womack, who served as my editor and marketing advisor.

Finally, I want to acknowledge John Berendt and the enormous impact his book, _"Midnight in the Garden of Good and Evil"_ had on Mother's celebrity and success as a musician, and on this story. The story of the Kellys would certainly have been possible without 'the book', but it would not have been nearly as compelling and nearly as far reaching. _"Midnight"_ changed the dynamic of the city of Savannah, Georgia, and changed the trajectory of Mother's career. John remained a close friend to Mother up until her death, and has continued to be a friend to our family to this day.

Introduction

The lights are low. Conversation drifts in and out. Couples lean toward each other. And there are the lonely searching the crowd for the blessing that harshly will never come their way...a pretty face, smiling back, thus turning their hungry souls onto a once dead carousel now making music, a melody of chance.

The Pope of this Papacy, the bar hop, makes a swish move of a mighty towel across this mahogany stage, just one more time. A tender moment for him as tears of the soloist baptizes the bar.

Music completes this snug cathedral. Music fulfilling. Music that lifts the pain from the lonely. Music that adds to the couple leaning. Quietly, the pianist, a lovely lady, drifting in her mid-sixties, begins to sing. Sultry. Low and so soft at the beginning. Everyone, regardless of emotional menu turns and listens. Oh, do they ever. She is quite something.

Her eyes are closed. Her hands grace the keys, as Van Gogh his brushes. With a touch classical. Soon her mastery and its magic surround the lounge – the lonely, the loving. The lady of the caressing the BLUES, her touch of genius as she blends the black and ivory and then her voice verging on the impossible to be that rare of implanting notes bring magic.

The singer, the pianist; this musical mood of those evenings are lifted up and forward by an angel – Emma Kelly. Ah, yes indeed, wherever this 'Lady of Six Thousand Songs' is present, that setting spins mightily bringing the holiness of a Chapel to the neon lights of Broadway.

Emma! Emma! How many know you? Thousands for sure! Your music over four decades has graced lounges, weekly Civic Club meetings, Dance Recitals, Weddings, Boy Scout Jamborees. Name any collections of human kind, and you have been there lifting high the purpose of such gathering.

Name it! She has played it! She is magnificent!

One fan calls her the John Wayne of music. "There ain't nothin' this fine lady can't do when it comes to a piano." Another salute from a retired military officer "She would play for us when we had no one. She'd come to the base to lift us as she sang good stuff. Oft' times she would invite us to sing with her. Emma was our home; our heart."

If the hundreds of little girls and boys Emma has accompanied during springtime Dance Recitals could be found, they would surly say "she would add magic to our planned steps. When we saw Ms. Emma across the stage lights, we knew we were safe. If we made a mistake this wonderful lady stayed with us dotting out musically our miscue."

Her concert of notes epitomizes the very light within. God blessed her with a talent she has given back to life each and every one of her days.

She and George had ten children. They reared them right. Each graduated high school and college. Emma was a pianist. George a sign painter. Together they provided a home of love and security.

Music by the grace of God and Emma were their lives. She encouraged them to join in. Play an instrument. Sing. Dance. "I truly enjoyed having my children with me when I performed."

Music is her life.

On any given day, she would drive to Lyons, Georgia for a Dance Recital; make a quick trip back through Statesboro to play for The Rotary Club, then on to Savannah for an evening with the loving, the lonely.

She is an institution.

She has lived in South Georgia all her life. Her music – sixty plus years of it – moves from the farmland onto the horizon of the world.

Florence, Italy - The Bridge Pointe Vecchio. One of the illustrated walk ways across the river. It is lined with gift stands. Stopping to admire an item alive with sunshine, a couple moving about this lovely storage commented. "We should take this to Emma Kelly. That looks just like something she would wear."

Yes, her music, sultry and blue coming from beneath those south Georgia pines onto the world. Emma, revered by parents of little children. Remembered by soldiers far from home. Her music is the face that smiles at the lonely—that gathers even closer the couples leaning, the bells of her ivories during Sunday School.

Emma, oh, you wonderful lady.

An encore please.

Just one!

Ric Mandes,

Noted columnist, essayists and author of five books. Written Circa 1987

Prologue

Small towns in the rural south in the early 1960's, were a mix of *'Ozzie and Harriet'* and *'Green Acres'*... soda fountains, sock hops, shag dancing and drive-in movies in town; cow tipping, bird hunting, square dancing, and farming in the country. That was certainly the case in Statesboro, Georgia. Our family lived in town, but we spent time with cousins, aunts and uncles in the country, so we knew both worlds.

We had little money, but we were too busy to know it. We went to school, attended church on Sundays, played sports and music, went to parties, worked part-time jobs, occasionally did homework, and in general, enjoyed life. But we had to work for every bit of it.

Our parents were busy, too. They worked virtually seven days a week to keep us fed, clothed, housed, and educated. In addition to tending to the needs of their children, they also had their careers and businesses to manage. They were just like any other Mom and Dad, and we were just like any other family growing up in South Georgia... only, well, bigger.

There were ten children in our family. When the average number of children in a family in the 1960's was 3 or 4, a family of ten children tends to stand out, especially in a small town like ours.

Our Mother was a piano player, who later became somewhat of a celebrity. She went from being the local pianist that played for church and Sunday school, anniversary parties, dance recitals, school plays and every other gig she could muster in and around town, to being featured in a New York Times best seller, followed by a cameo appearance in a major Hollywood movie. She was even given a stage name, *"The Lady of 6,000 Songs."*

My nine brothers and sisters and I performed song and dance routines as part our mother's musical performances. We became known as the large musical family from Statesboro, Georgia.

Despite those modest distinctions, however, we felt no different from anyone else in our hometown. We had two independent and hard-working parents, with little or no money, who raised their ten children by scraping and clawing a living from sign painting and piano playing. In the end, we became ten children who would all grow up to get college degrees, enjoy good health, prosperity, and a closeness that we would not fully appreciate or understand until later in life.

We never gave it much thought even when Mother began to experience some degree of fame and notoriety from her piano playing. Nor did it seem extraordinary when she was featured in a best-selling book. Even when she was cast to portray herself in a motion picture directed by Clint Eastwood, it just didn't seem to be that big of a deal. It was only after we lost Mother and Dad and had children and grandchildren of our own, that we begin to put our experience into some context. It was only after our children and grandchildren, many of whom would never know their grandparents, began to ask questions, that we began to get it.

Our children and grandchildren seemed to see the unusual nature of our lives growing up before we did. It was their questions about our large and rather unique family that gave the ten of us a perspective that we were probably too close to see on our own. It was also their questions that served as the catalyst for this book.

This book is written in memory of my Mother and Father, and for any and every one that knew or had met George or Emma Kelly and appreciated the character and strength of the two of them.

It is written for our many friends in Statesboro and Bulloch County and Savannah and South Georgia who knew our family, and had a helping hand in guiding us, supporting us, and at times praying for us.

It is written for every parent that knows firsthand the challenges of raising a family while trying to manage their own lives and careers, and their marriage.

It is written for everyone who has a love of music, and for musicians everywhere who know firsthand the challenges of trying to be heard, or trying to make it in what is perhaps the most competitive industry known to mankind.

It is written for the spouses and in-laws that married into the Kelly family, who thought they understood what they were marrying into, only to realize after it was too late, that they did not. They loved and supported us anyway.

But most of all, this book is written for my children and grandchildren, and the children and grandchildren of my brothers and sisters... many of whom never met or got to know their grandparents or great-grandparents. They are the ones who have heard and read the stories about the rag-tag, helter-skelter, magical musical tour that was the Kellys, but never fully understood or appreciated what it really meant.

It is written in hopes that they will develop a little better understanding of who George and Emma Kelly were, and what life was like with the two of them and their ten children, in a glorious time, and a glorious place.

PART 1

Before There Was a "Lady of 6,000 Songs"

A $3 Bet...

William Aiken Williams grew up in the low country of Allendale, South Carolina in the early 1900's. His father was a successful farmer, and though he divorced his wife and moved to Florida, he left a comfortable life behind for his family. His mother was a woman who appreciated the finer things in life and expected the same for her children, especially her only son, Aiken.

Aiken Williams was a larger than life character. He was attractive, witty, unfailingly mischievous, and accustomed to getting his way. Even as an adult, he was continually doted on by his mother, and like his father, he struggled with the demons of alcohol.

After serving in the Spanish-American war, Williams returned to his family's farming business and became a successful farmer and businessman.

In 1902, he married Sarah Pauline Cave, a local schoolteacher who was educated and classically trained in music and the arts at nearby Winthrop College. She was petite, charming, and refined in her demeanor, but possessed an inner strength of her character and her convictions.

In the first ten years of their marriage, the couple produced six children and were expecting a seventh. While his wife devoted herself to the development of their children, Williams devoted his time to his farm and a local 'spirits' store he owned, which served as a convenient gathering spot for many of the other farmers and locals in the area. His store was not only popular as a local hangout for refreshments, the backroom of the establishment also served as the site for regular poker games, which Williams hosted after hours.

After long, hot summer days in the fields, land owners and sharecroppers alike invariably found their way to his store for their daily refreshments and on occasion, try their hand at the poker table. It was not uncommon to see wagons and horses tied up outside the dusty establishment well into the night, long after they should have been back in the barn readying for the next day of farming.

Aiken Williams' customers usually paid in cash, but on those occasions when they needed a little credit, Williams gladly accommodated them. It was not that he was a generous man willing to help a friend in need. In fact, some said it was just the opposite. He enjoyed having his customers indebted to him. That was always a good position to be in when he needed a special favor, or when the stakes got high during one of his poker games.

Lonnie Tillman was a local sharecropper and a regular at Mr. William's store and at his back room poker games. Over time, Lonnie had run up his share of debt to Mr. Williams, both in bad liquor and bad cards, and he had grown accustomed to the store owner's ridicule and taunts about his debts. Tillman did not like Aiken Williams, and he certainly didn't like being indebted to the man.

'Dirt poor' was a good description of Lonnie Tillman, even in the best of times. With no money to speak of, and a growing debt, Lonnie's only hope of freeing himself from the stranglehold would be a streak of good luck at the poker table. He knew that would be the only way he could ever pay off his liquor tab and get Aiken Williams off his back. One cold night in December 1913, it appeared that his moment may have arrived.

Even in the moderate climate of South Carolina, winters could be cold, especially when working outside on the farms all day. Cold, raw winter days made the warmth of Mr. Williams' poker games even more alluring at night. His store had the largest wood burning stove in the area, and even when they had a bad night at the poker table, the liquor and the warmth of the stove kept farmers there, many times late into the night.

On this December night, the game started early. By nightfall, the table was crowded and the wood burning stove was cranking out the heat. The cards and the liquor flowed freely as the flames from the stove and the kerosene lanterns merged with the haze of cigar smoke to give the room an eerie glow.

It was a rare occurrence, but on this night, Lonnie Tillman was having a good run of cards. Usually on the losing end, the sight of a large pile of money and chips in front of him was an unusual site and began to make him nervous. He decided to quit while he was ahead. He would collect his winnings and call it a night.

Aiken Williams did not like losing, and he did not want to see Lonnie Tillman walk out with his winnings, or his freedom from the chokehold of debt that the store owner held over his head. So, he made the sharecropper a final proposition.

The two of them would play one last hand, which would give Lonnie Tillman the opportunity to gain even bigger winnings… or lose it all. Reluctantly Tillman agreed to the proposition, and the game began. The cards and the liquor continued to flow, and the betting was more furious than anyone could remember.

As the final cards were dealt, all of the money that Lonnie Tillman had won that evening was no longer in front of him, but now in the pot in the middle of the table. He had no more money to bet, and Aiken Williams knew it. He had the perpetual loser right where he wanted him.

To force the issue and Lonnie Tillman's hand, Williams made a final bet for $3. He knew Tillman could not match the bet, which would mean him forfeiting the game, and all of his winnings.

Feeling cornered and cheated, Lonnie Tillman flew into a rage. Cursing uncontrollably, he flipped over the table, and as cards, money and poker

5

chips went flying, he retrieved a revolver from his boot and shot Aiken Williams dead.

Lonnie Tillman had no standing in the local South Carolina community, and was easily convicted of murder., but Aiken Williams was no more. While there were those in the community that may have sympathized with Tillman, Williams' wife, Pauline and their six children, seemingly overnight, were thrown from a life of comfort, to a life of total disarray.

Pauline Williams was five months pregnant when her husband was killed. Now widowed, she sent her children to live with their grandmother in Savannah, and other family members in Miami Florida, while she prepared to give birth to her seventh child and try to get her life re-established.

After her son was born, whom she would name Paul, she moved to Guyton, Georgia, outside of Savannah, to go back to doing what she loved most... teaching school. The classically trained pianist and educator once again had the opportunity to indulge her passion, until fate would intervene once again, three years later.

Pauline had a cousin, Anna Morris, who lived in nearby Leefield, Georgia, a small farming community outside of the county seat of Statesboro. Like Pauline, Anna Morris was also married to a farmer and general store owner. Her husband's name was Willie Thompson, and they, too, had six children.

Three years after Aiken Williams was killed over a $3 bet in a poker game, Anna Morris died, and left her husband, Willie Thompson, a widower with their six children to tend to.

He remarried quickly, but within a year, his second wife also died.

Within a year after his second wife's death, Willie Thompson was introduced to and married Pauline Williams, in what she later described as a 'marriage of convenience.' She moved into his farm in Leefield GA, where she would take up her new life with her new husband and their combined families.

Several children from their previous marriages were still living elsewhere with relatives, so the newly married couple only had seven of their children living with them on the farm in Leefield.

But there would be more to come.

Less than a year after their marriage, Pauline Thompson, gave birth to her first child with her new husband… a daughter they would name Emma Sease Thompson.

Through these many twists and turns of life, death, marriage and a $3 bet, Willie Thompson and Pauline Williams Thompson would become our grandparents, and Emma Thompson would become our Mother. Were it not for that $3 bet between Aiken Williams and Lonnie Tillman, the story of the life, music and family of Emma Kelly, would have never happened.

There was yet, another piece of the puzzle that would be essential to this story… and it would have its share of twists and turns as well.

The Barber from Tennessee

Frank Kelley (spelled with an 'e') was a native of Chattanooga Tennessee. He would become the father of George Kelly, and the grandfather to the ten children George and Emma Kelly would produce, but he would never know his son, or his son's large family. He would remain the biggest mystery in the annals of the Kelly family, and though the spelling would change, his name would be forever linked to the story and the history of George and Emma Kelly.

Frank Kelley found his way to Statesboro GA sometime in 1911. He found work as a barber and took up residence in a local boarding house. Being an outsider, he had no ties to the community, and he developed few friends or acquaintances outside of his work. He did, however, manage to catch the eye of one O'phelia 'Phoebe' Beasley.

The contrast of her being a life-long resident of the community, born into a well-established family of Bulloch County civic and political leaders and Frank Kelley being a newcomer in the community did not go unnoticed. O'phelia was the 7th of 13 children born to George Ross and Sarah Ann Beasley. Her father was a farmer, and her grandfather was a local politician, having at one time served as the tax collector for Bulloch County.

She was thirty-one years old when she met Frank Kelley, and still lived at home with her parents. She had never been married and never had a serious relationship to speak of. In the early 1900's, being over thirty and unmarried, O'phelia Beasley would have been characterized as an 'old maid.' She did not possess strikingly good looks, and had a disposition that was at times, described as gruff, so it is fair to wonder what attracted Frank Kelley to O'phelia Beasley. Future events might suggest he was not so much attracted to O'phelia Beasley, but to the potential benefits of being connected to her large, extended family.

The two met at a social gathering in late 1911. He was charming and flirtatious, and not being accustomed to attention from male suitors, she was flattered and awkwardly receptive to his charms. They began a courtship that by turn of the century standards, was considered 'fast and furious.' Less than six months after they met, on April 6, 1912, the two entered into a marriage that would last less than one year.

Within the first month of their marriage, the newlywed Mrs. Kelley became pregnant with their first child. Seven months later, however, her husband was gone. Frank Kelley supposedly went on a business trip back to his home in Chattanooga, Tennessee, but was never seen or heard from again. While some suspected foul play, the family ultimately concluded the man simply had given up on whatever gains he thought he might realize from his marriage into the Beasley family, and abandoned his pregnant wife in search of a better life elsewhere.

After her husband's disappearance, Phoebe Beasley Kelley returned to live with her father and mother, George Ross and Rebecca Beasley, and prepared for the birth of her child, and on February 5th, 1913, a son was born. She would name him George Ross Kelley, named for his maternal grandfather, and with the surname of a father he would never know.

George R.

With a large extended family surrounding him, George R., as he came to be called, experienced a relatively normal childhood, despite the absence of a father. He had an outgoing personality, a keen sense of humor and was described by classmates and friends as a joker and prankster. He received an abundance of attention from his mother and extended family, and an abundance of strict parental guidance as well. His personality, however, was carefree and free spirited in nature, and the strict guidance did not always stick. As he described his adolescence, "I didn't break all the rules, but I certainly bent a few."

George Kelley enjoyed life.

In the classroom, he was a marginal student and somewhat indifferent to academics. He had an uncanny knack for drawing, and when he was supposed to be studying math or science, he spent his time doodling and drawing airplanes or buildings and other creations that were in his head. Though his interest in academics was minimal, he did have an ambitious side when it came to his affinity for drawing and painting. He did freelance work as a teenager, drawing posters and small signs for store owners and shopkeepers around town, which began to set the foundation for having his own sign business. He was also intrigued with the emerging novelty of airplanes. He was 14 when Charles Lindbergh made his historic flight across the Atlantic, and from that moment, he was forever captivated by his love of flying.

After graduating from high school in 1929, at the time of the stock market crash and the dawn of the Great Depression, he attended Georgia Teachers College in Statesboro, which, at the time, was a two year institution before eventually becoming Georgia Southern University.

In his second year at the school, he concluded college was not for him, and he embarked on his sign painting business, which was far more interesting to him than academia. Despite the financial hardships that prevailed in the 1930's, he found enough work to keep him busy and convince him that he could actually make a living painting signs for local businesses in the area.

It was during this time that he also found something else... a local farm community not far from town where a young lady had captured his attention.

Emma Thompson

Growing up on her family's farm in Leefield, some ten miles from Statesboro, Emma loved the country and she loved horseback riding. But her true love was the piano.

Willie and Pauline Thompson had a beautiful piano in the parlor of their home, which he had bought for his new bride as a wedding present. One day, while working in the kitchen, Pauline heard someone striking keys on the piano in a deliberate attempt to pick out a tune. Slowly, she recognized the tune....

"Jesus loves me, this I know. For the Bible tells me so..."

Pauline was surprised to discover three year-old Emma at the keys. The toddler had dragged a stool into the parlor so that she could climb onto the piano bench. Her daughter was a natural, and Pauline committed herself to nurturing her daughter's talent. She spent countless hours teaching her basic chords and arranging formal lessons from other teachers. Within months of that discovery, Emma was performing for family and friends, and by the age of nine, she was performing regularly in church and for social events in the community.

Emma's talent as a pianist not only gave her a sense of purpose, it also afforded her privileges that her brothers and sisters did not enjoy. She showed a distinct lack of enthusiasm for the chores that went with her family's sprawling farm, and while her siblings were taking care of chores, Emma was usually inside practicing the piano or performing. It was one of those performances that brought her together with her future husband.

George and Emma Come Together

Mother and Dad first met at a church function, and according to friends, he was immediately smitten with the much younger piano player. She was an attractive teenager from the country with dark, flowing hair and an engaging personality. Dad was a tall, lanky college boy from town, who possessed a quick wit and an easy smile. He was more than five years her senior, but they developed an attraction for each other and engaged in an off and on courtship that lasted throughout Mother's high school years. Mother was flattered by his pursuit and enjoyed her time with him, but at the same time, she liked keeping her options open.

When Mother graduated from high school, Dad made his case for marriage. It took several attempts before he won her over, but he finally did. His persistence eventually paid off when, against the wishes of her family, on May 19th, 1936, the two drove across the Georgia state line to Ridgeland, South Carolina where they were married. He was twenty-three; she was seventeen.

Mom and Dad began their lives together in the midst of the Great Depression, under their new name, George R. and Emma **Kelly**.

Sometime before the 1930 census, Dad was told by his mother that she had changed their name from 'Kelley' to 'Kelly', and that he should drop the 'e' from his last name. It was her way of further separating herself and her son from her first husband and his name, and perhaps a way of strengthening the hope of a new life for herself. So it was that Emma Thompson married George R. **Kelly**.

The newly married and newly named couple set up house in a small apartment in Statesboro where Dad continued his sign painting business. Like everyone in those times, especially those just starting out, they struggled to make ends meet. The country was in the depths of the Great Depression, and fortunately for Dad, despite the desperate nature of the times, businesses were still willing to advertise. From storefront signs to company logos on the sides of their trucks to billboards on the sides of country roads, companies looked for ways to generate business in hard economic times. All of which helped Dad eke out a living as a sign painter. His work paid reasonably well when he could get it, but it was unpredictable. He worked nonstop painting signs and doing anything else he could to support himself and his wife.

Meanwhile, Mother took any odd job she could find, and on rare occasions, she was able to make a little side money playing the piano for church and school functions to contribute what she could.

They were fortunate to have come from large supportive families who helped the couple out when they could, but those early days of struggle made an indelible imprint on Mother.

She learned quickly how to make a little go a long way. She threw away nothing, and any form of edible food would invariably find its way into a skillet or pot in the form of a creative dish. These were skills and habits that would serve her well later in life as the mother of a large family.

"You Must Have Been a Beautiful Baby!"

Starting a family in the 1930's was a challenge. Jobs and money were scarce, and seemingly every waking moment was devoted to making ends meet. That challenge would become even greater for them, because they were about to start a family.

A little more than eight months into their marriage, Mother became pregnant for the first time. They had not planned or anticipated a baby at this stage in their marriage, but neither seemed to object to the idea. Though much of it took place during a typically hot and steamy South Georgia summer, her pregnancy was largely uneventful and she seemed to endure it well. She delivered her first baby without incident.

On September 27th, 1937, she gave birth to a beautiful daughter, whom they named Kitty. When asked later why she was named Kitty, Dad simply said he 'liked the name', and did not want to detract from it with a middle name.

Kitty had her father's disposition and her mother's talent and passion for the piano. Dad said Kitty talked 'early and often.' She was described as an active and precocious toddler, and almost immediately began to display her inherited talents. She began picking out tunes on the piano by age 3, and would grow cultivate her talents as a pianist and vocalist throughout her life.

At a time when the country was obsessing over the disappearance of aviatrix Amelia Earhart and her ill-fated effort to become the first person to fly around the world, Kitty's birth launched the first phase of the Kelly hit parade.

I should warn you, however, to hold on to your hats… from this point forward, this train is going to move at a pretty good clip.

A little more than two years later, on February 6, 1940, daughter #2 was born. Sarah Phoebe Kelly was named for Dad's mother, O'phelia, and provided Dad a nice birthday present. She was born the day after his 27th birthday.

In contrast to Kitty, Phoebe was described as much more reserved. She did not gravitate to the piano as her mother and older sister had done, but she did indeed have musical gifts, which would show up later in her life as a musician and dancer.

Phoebe was born at a time when the country was on the verge of war. Germany had invaded Poland, and in the Pacific, Japan had begun hostilities with virtually all of its Asian neighbors. On both fronts, America's entry into battle seemed only a matter of time. Phoebe was less than two years old when the Japanese attacked Pearl Harbor in December of 1941.

Pearl Harbor changed everything. The country was thrust into war and every family in the country would feel the impact of the sacrifices that accompanied war. Dad was not a prospect for the military draft because of his age and his family, but he did serve his country. He became a mail pilot for the War Department, which not only gave him a way to serve his country, but also allowed him to fulfill his lifelong dream to fly. He also served in the Merchant Marines, which sent him to Bermuda during the war.

The war, however, did not stop or even slow down the Kelly baby train. At the time of Phoebe's birth, there was no indication that a trend was beginning to develop, but a trend was definitely in the making. Just two years after Phoebe was born, daughter #3 arrived.

On May 29th, 1942, in the midst of some of the country's most difficult struggles of the war, Jacqueline Elizabeth Kelly, was born. Named for two of Mother's sisters, Jackie was born at a time when Mother and Dad both were doing their part in support of the war effort. Dad was working with the Merchant Marines, stationed in Bermuda, and Mother was working in the local shipyards in nearby Savannah, while Jackie and her two older sisters were cared for by their Grandmother.

Like her sisters, however, Jackie enjoyed her tenure as the baby of the family about as long as Kitty and Phoebe enjoyed theirs. In the six years they had been married, Mother and Dad had produced three girls in consecutive two-year intervals. This pattern would continue through the duration of the War and beyond.

As the country produced guns, airplanes and tanks in support of the war effort, the Kelly's produced daughters. Just one month shy of Jackie's 2nd birthday, on April 10th, 1944, Paula Carolyn Kelly was born.

Like Jackie, Paula was also named for one of Emma's many siblings, and like her sisters, Paula was born during an extraordinary time in history. The war in Europe was reaching a critical point, and the allied invasion of Europe and D-Day were only months away.

The four girls were cute, cuddly, and engaging, and Mother and Dad proudly showed them off to their friends and families. Even at their young ages, Mother was beginning to envision the ancillary benefits of having a group of attractive, talented daughters.

Emma, the USO and Fort Stewart: A Musical Marriage Made in Heaven

Mother and Dad were raising a family in the midst of shortages, embargoes and all the other restrictions the country had imposed in support the war effort. Dad continued his stint in the Merchant Marines and Mother continued to work as an assembly worker in the local shipyards in Savannah, while at the same time looking for any and every opportunity she could find to play the piano.

Hello USO.

When the country went to war, the military looked for ways to entertain the troops and maintain their morale while they were stationed in foreign lands. In 1941, the War Department created the United Services Organization, or USO, to do just that.

It was the USO that sponsored dances and other social gatherings to entertain the troops during their training or when they were home on leave from the war. It was the USO that recruited entertainers like Benny Goodman and Glenn Miller to visit military installations around the world to perform for the troops who were stationed in war zones. It was the USO that dispatched Bob Hope and his vaudeville troupe around the world to entertain troops during World War II, and later Korea, Viet Nam and wherever else American troops were doing battle. And it was the USO that turned Mother's piano playing from a casual part-time endeavor into a full-time musical career.

Up until this time, Mother's piano playing activities consisted mostly of performing for weddings, anniversary parties, and small dances in and around Statesboro. The jobs were small and the money was smaller, and while her heart would always remain with those local performances, she knew that if she were to ever make money with her talent, she would have to take it beyond the confines of Statesboro and Bulloch County. The opportunity to do just that was presented to her when she met a woman named Mary Lazenby, who was the head of the USO at nearby Fort Stewart in Hinesville, Georgia.

Fort Stewart was located about 40 miles from Statesboro, and had become a major training facility for the Army during the war.

The hot steamy climate and the heavy underbrush of South Georgia provided ideal training conditions for soldiers who prepared to face combat in Europe, Africa and in the Pacific.

Thousands of recruits and officers passed through the military base in preparation for combat, and it was Mary Lazenby's job to look for ways to entertain the troops to offset the isolation and drudgery of their training. It was Mary Lazenby's job to find local talent to come to the base and put on performances, and Mary Lazenby found just the person to do the job... Emma Kelly!

Mother began performing with a small all-female combo, which became an instant hit with the predominantly male audiences. Soldiers from all over the country who found themselves stuck on a small isolated military base in the swamps of South Georgia, found in Emma Kelly, someone who knew their favorite song.

They found someone that, through her music, could remind them of home. They found someone who made the inconveniences of military life a little more bearable.

Mother, in turn, found in the USO, an opportunity to become a full-time entertainer, and make money doing something she truly loved. She was talented enough to play all of the hits of the day, and she was savvy enough to give her audience what they wanted.

It was the perfect marriage.

As her popularity grew, so did her opportunities to perform. She was soon driving to Ft. Stewart five, six, and sometimes seven days a week. Her activities ranged from Tuesday and Thursday sing-along's at the Services Club, to Friday night dances at the Non-Commissioned Officer's Club, to formal dances on Saturday night at the Officer's Club, to playing background music at Sunday afternoon socials. Whatever Ft. Stewart needed in the way of entertainment, Mother was determined to provide it, never forgetting the cardinal rule of show business, *"give 'em what they want."*

No matter the function and no matter the form of entertainment requested, Mother was there. She knew the music of the popular big bands of the era. She had the ability to pull musicians together to form a band. She knew how to engage a crowd, and soon she had become one of Fort Stewart's most popular and reliable entertainers.

Her performances at Ft. Stewart in Hinesville introduced her to other USO opportunities elsewhere in the area. She was soon performing for the USO at nearby Hunter AFB in Savannah, and Ft. Gordon in Augusta, and Ft. Benning in Columbus, Ft. Jackson in South Carolina, and any other military installation in the area in need of entertainment. Soon, she and her combo were traveling to these locations almost every Friday and Saturday night entertaining troops and military dignitaries.

The USO at Fort Stewart GA provided Mother the start of a musical career that would enable her to devote herself to her music, and be an active contributor to the family finances. With her growing family and her increasing opportunities to play music, this was the beginning of a juggling act between her music and her family that would continue for the next twenty years.

Thus " The Emma Kelly Combo"

The Baby Boom Continues...

As World War II came to an end with the surrender of Germany and Japan, thousands of GI's returned home from the war to begin rebuilding their lives and their families. This massive return of military veterans brought about the largest influx of marriages, pregnancies, and new baby's in the country's history, and this would spawn what would become known as "The Baby Boom" era.

Mother and Dad were happy to do their part with their own baby boom. Paula's time as 'the baby' of the family would last about as long as her three older sisters. Staying true to the pattern that was established with the first four, Mother became pregnant again in the fall of 1945 with what would be Kelly number five. After four consecutive girls, what should anyone expect but another girl. But as the couple's friends would describe, they were both surprised and delighted that on April 26th, 1946, they would have their first son.
That would be me. I would be named George Ross Kelly, Jr.

I was the first boy in the family after four consecutive girls, and according to the records, I was the largest of the Kelly children at birth, tipping the scales at just over 10 lbs. I grew up thinking I had five mothers, as it seemed I was taken care of and told what to do by each of my sisters, as well as Mother.

With five children now to support, Mom and Dad continued to scrape for everything they could get to take care of their growing family. The post-war economy was gaining strength, and Dad's sign business remained steady. But a family of seven had a lot of needs, and the couple did anything and everything they could to provide for their growing family.

Thanks to the USO and Fort Stewart, Mother had begun to actually make money through her music. It seemed, however, whatever gains were made were usually offset by the demands of their growing family. And grow it did.

In the fall of 1948, I was two years old when Mother became pregnant again. This would be Kelly number six, but this one would be bitter-sweet for the couple.

Frederick Beasley was Dad's cousin. The two were similar in age and grew up together. Fred was the closest thing Dad had to a brother and remained close to both Dad and Mother. In the fall of 1948, Fred Beasley went on a fishing trip on the Canadian side of Lake Michigan. During one of the outings, the boat he was on capsized, and he drowned.

Dad's best friend and closest relative was gone.

Fred's body was not immediately recovered, and with the winter coming and Canada's lakes freezing over, the search for bodies was suspended until the following spring.

The search for Fred's body resumed the following April, at a time when Mother and Dad were preparing for Kelly #6. On May 4th, 1949, Frederick's body was recovered from the bottom of Lake Michigan, the same day that Mother gave birth to a second son.

In honor of their cousin, he was named William Frederick Kelly.

Though he was clearly a boy, Bill was deemed pretty enough to be girl, and for reasons only his four older sisters and Mother could explain, Bill's hair went uncut until he was three years old. He had an angelic face and golden curly shoulder length hair, and while we knew him to be a boy, his photographs as a three year old could convince anyone outside the family that he was the prettiest little girl you had ever seen.

Bill and I were the only two boys with four older sisters, and despite his golden locks, we played endlessly together. We didn't know it at the time, but we would soon have even more playmates. Bill's birth was the starting point for the most rapid fire series of new additions to the family. Just fifteen months after Bill was born, Kelly number seven was welcomed into the world… this time, another girl.

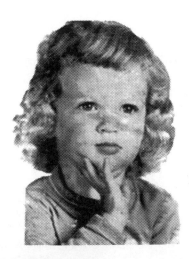

On August 27, 1950, Emaline became the fifth daughter to join her older sisters. She provided the older girls a new baby sister to entertain and spoil, and with another girl in the family, Bill and I were feeling more and more outnumbered, and in even greater need to stick together as brothers.

It wouldn't be long, however, before we got reinforcements. Just sixteen months after Emaline was born, on December 7th, 1951, Michael David Kelly became the eighth Kelly and the third Kelly son. Mike enjoyed a unique place in the birth order, and a distinction none of his brothers and sisters before him experienced. He spent almost five years as the 'baby' of the family.

By this time, whatever semblance of normalcy and calm might have ever existed in the Kelly household was clearly gone. In addition to the sheer numbers of children, three of them were still toddlers, leaving Mother and the older sisters very busy taking care of their younger siblings. Long before the days of disposable diapers and pre-mixed baby formulas, the household was littered with lots of babies, lots of milk, lots of baby bottles, lots of toys, and lots of diapers to be changed and washed.

Now for those of you who are trying desperately to keep up and need a moment to catch your breath, I will attempt to provide some context at this point...

At the time Mike was born...

- Kitty was thirteen
- Phoebe was eleven
- Jackie was nine
- Paula was seven
- I was five
- Bill was not yet three, and
- Emaline was not yet two.

The baby train was moving faster than ever, Mother was performing more, and Dad was working more and more with his sign painting business. More bodies were doing more things, going more places, at a faster pace. A new normal was beginning to take shape.

With Mother and Dad increasingly pre-occupied with the business of supporting the family, Kitty, Phoebe, Jackie and Paula began to assume the lion's share of the household chores and the care for their younger siblings. A practice began to take shape in the family in which each of the older sisters 'adopted' one or more of their younger siblings, as their primary overseer. The younger children grew up with a very busy mother and father and four doting, but demanding older sisters who acted as surrogate parents.

This group parenting process, while not necessarily recommended by child psychologists or childcare experts, proved to not only be functional, but was instrumental in creating the bond among the ten of us that would last a lifetime.

A Time to Pause and Reflect

After Mike was born, there was a span of almost five years on the baby front without a new addition... which was a record for Mother and Dad. But, as Paul Harvey used to say, *'and now the rest of the story...'*

Between 1951 and 1955, Mother lost three babies in succession to miscarriages, and again, I'll pause to let you contemplate what our family would have looked like, had she brought any of them to full term. This was a time when she and Dad were busier than ever, a time when the older girls were beginning to have lives of their own, and a time in which the world around us was changing.

The great depression had come and gone. Germany, Italy and Japan had been defeated to bring World War II to a successful conclusion. The Korean War was coming to an end, and the post-war economic boom of the 1950's was cranking up. The average household salary at the time was just under $3,000 a year.

At a time when the world was discovering rock and roll, Mother was going strong with the old standards and big band hits of the 1930's and 40's. She had built a growing following as a pianist and orchestra leader performing in clubs and dance halls around the area, as well as her continued work with the USO.

The older Kelly children were becoming teenagers and learning to balance their responsibilities as surrogate mothers and performers with their efforts to be normal teenagers. They went from washing diapers, to tap dance routines, to poodle skirts and sock hops, all in a matter of a day.

Dad's sign business was growing, fueled by the increase in tourists traveling to and from Florida which called for an increase in roadside signs and billboards up and down US Highway 301 seeking their business. In many respects, Dad was a typical southerner. He enjoyed the jokes about 'Yankees', but his was one of the many businesses that benefitted from the Yankee tourists. He was working six and seven days a week, and amazingly, he also managed to find a way to continue his love of flying.

The 1950's marked the beginning of what became known as the Cold War. The political divide between the democratic policies of the US and Western Europe, and the communist policies of the Soviet Union and Eastern Europe created a climate of paranoia, mistrust and nuclear gamesmanship. Both sides were developing and producing nuclear weapons capabilities, and with the overriding fear of a nuclear holocaust, both sides built a culture and a defense infrastructure to deter and prepare for nuclear attack.

In support of the civil defense of the country, during these times of fear and paranoia, the US government created an auxiliary Air Force agency called the Civil Air Patrol. The agency served to augment the country's air defense by organizing civilian pilots to be available in the event of an emergency. Local chapters were chartered to support their local communities in air search and rescue missions, and, in general, to champion and promote the interests of pilots and flying. If you could design an ideal hobby and diversion for Dad from the challenges of his business and raising a family, the Civil Air Patrol would be it. He was an active member for over twenty years, and eventually became the local Commander.

Mother, meanwhile, continued her regular routine at Ft. Stewart, but she also began to branch out beyond the military to play for business conventions, government organizations, politicians and other functions that extended her musical reach.

With the absence of new babies, a post-war economy and an older, seemingly more manageable household, the first half of the 1950's was a time of relative calm and routine for the family. Though the cold war was in full swing, and issues like Sputnik, McCarthyism, and the communist scare dominated the news headlines, this was a time when it seemed the country could actually relax and breathe from the years of war and depression.

That was true for the Mom and Dad and the family as well. However, that would soon change.

The Fire

Christmas of 1955 was a busy holiday season for Mother. She performed for Christmas parties almost every night during the month of December, leading up to her busiest and most lucrative night of the year, New Year's Eve. Following three miscarriages in the past three years, she was pregnant once again during the holidays of 1955, but that did not slow her down from her performances.

I was nine years old and got my first bicycle that Christmas. It was a Huffy, red with white trim, and it had a small book rack on the rear wheel, which I assumed was meant to transport a passenger. I rode it constantly for the first couple of days, and guarded it with my life when I wasn't riding it. I couldn't tell you what any of my brothers or sisters got for Christmas that year. I was too preoccupied with my first bicycle.

One night after the Christmas break, I went to spend the night with our grandmother Phoebe (Dad's mother), which was a common practice for us at the time. The number of kids in our house always exceeded the number of beds, which meant we were always sharing a bed with one or more of our brothers or sisters. So a night at Grandmother's gave us the rare opportunity to sleep in our own bed, a luxury we seldom experienced.

Grandmother lived in a small apartment on South College Street. She did not have a television, and the radio was generally an afterthought. As a result, our time with her was usually spent reading or talking, or finding other ways to entertain ourselves. We generally looked forward to the occasion when it was our turn to stay at Grandmother's, and on this occasion, it was an opportunity to talk about the Christmas holidays... and my new bicycle.

Our evening was uneventful, and as usual, we went to bed around 9:30 or 10:00 o'clock. Enjoying my evening of solitude with no brothers kicking me in the night, I drifted into a deep and peaceful sleep. That is, until about 2:00 o'clock in the morning.

Grandmother and I were jarred awake by a loud commotion outside and pounding on the door. Once we recovered from our initial disorientation, we found our way to the door to discover Mother and all of my brothers and sisters, wrapped in blankets and forging their way inside to escape the cold. I remember little of what was said in the chaos of those first few moments, and I remember absolutely nothing after hearing the words, *"The house caught fire. It has burned down."*

Needless to say, my night of solitude with Grandmother was gone.

Our house was completely destroyed, along with all of our possessions and our new Christmas gifts... including my new bicycle.

In the chaos of getting everyone out safely, Dad could not find Paula or me, not remembering that she was spending the night with Donna Minkovitz, and I with Grandmother. He suffered minor burns in the process of getting everyone out safely, but given the potential of injury and death that could have resulted, we were very fortunate that it was not worse.

It was concluded that an oil burner used to heat the house was the culprit, and ignited some materials that rapidly spread throughout the house. Along with Dad, our dog, Rusty, was the hero of the moment, as it was his barking that initially alerted everyone to the fire.

With no insurance, we were left with nothing... nothing except our lives.

The days, weeks and months that followed that chaotic night proved to be the most challenging in Mothers and Dad's lives. It also proved to be a time when we as a family discovered the depth of love and generosity expressed by our hometown. We were a family in need, and Statesboro and its outlying communities responded.

Eight children needed to be tended to as Mother and Dad went about the business of finding us a new home and rebuilding our lives. We needed a place to live. We needed clothes. We needed furnishings, appliances, and all the incidentals that had been lost, which was everything we owned. As Mother and Dad went into action, so did the community.

For starters, where do you put eight children? While Mother and Dad and some of the children stayed with family members, others of us became extended houseguests with friends. Jackie, Phoebe and Kitty stayed with Grandmother. Paula stayed with the Robert and Jewell (and Owen and Judy) Zetterower family and with Donna Minkovitz. I also stayed with the Minkovitz's for a while, with Donna's brother, David, and Paula and I both benefitted from the generosity and the wardrobes of David and Donna.

A vacant storefront on West Main Street next to Banks Dairy was set up as a central receiving area for donations of household goods, which included pots, pans, clothing, furnishings, and other essentials required to rebuild our lives. Our grandmother's apartment served as another receiving area where we received food, clothes, and other essentials. The First Baptist Church raised money and donations on behalf of the family.

It was all a blur for us, but we were in dire straits, and the people of Statesboro and Bulloch County responded in a big way. None of us will ever forget that experience, and we will never forget the generosity of our community at a time when we needed it most.

Shortly after the fire, we moved into a small 2-3 bedroom apartment, while Dad remodeled a home he had purchased on South College Street. In addition to getting the house ready for our large family, he was also determined to ensure that the house would have safe exit routes in the event of another fire.

43

The two story, four bedroom house was expanded to five bedrooms; and each bedroom had a floor to ceiling closet area, which created the effect of having two semi-private bedrooms in one. For the first time in our childhoods, we had our own bedroom, or at least the effect of our own bedroom.

Fire retardant paint was used on all the ceilings and walls to minimize the spread of fire. Balconies were built outside of each bedroom, to ensure a rapid and safe exit in the event of fire or other emergency. If there was a silver lining in the loss of our house and all of our possessions in the fire, it was that the new house provided Dad the opportunity to apply his creative architectural and design skills to create the home that he had always wanted us to have.

The new house became Dad's lifetime obsession. He spent many nights in his easy chair drawing and re-drawing the next innovation that he wanted to add. Our new home was a continual work-in-progress of both interior and exterior renovations, and a continual source of challenge and enjoyment for Dad.

It was there at 445 South College Street that the family would spend the remaining days of our childhoods. It was there that we grew up with neighbors and classmates that would remain lifelong friends. The Cooks lived next door. The Stephens lived next to them. They, like the Curlins, Russells, Franklins, Mathis', Altmans, Keiths, Ellis', Scruggs', Rogers, Turners, and our high school math teacher, Velma Kemp, would be the friends and neighbors that were closest to the vortex that was the Kelly whirlwind.

It was there that Mother and Dad would remain until, as empty nesters, they moved into a condominium, at which time, the house was divided into apartment units, which remain today as college housing.

The fire that destroyed our home and all of our possessions provided Dad the opportunity to build the house he wanted, and it also solidified the family's appreciation and love affair with the people of Statesboro and Bulloch County. They were there at a time when we needed them most.

Baby Boom, Part 3

The lull in babies from Mother's miscarriages may have been God's way of saying to Mom and Dad:

> *"Relax. Take a break. Rest up. There is a lot going on. There will be more time for babies."*

Divine intervention or not, they were not convinced. They adhered to the old adage, *"if at once you don't succeed, try and try again!"* And try again they did.

Following her three miscarriages, Mother was again pregnant when the house was destroyed by fire, and this time she would be successfully deliver Kelly number nine. Peter Franklin Kelly ('Pete') was born on July 23rd, 1956, and took his place as the fourth Kelly boy to join his five sisters.

Given the disruption from the fire, Pete was born at a time of transition for the family. He came home to a temporary, but crowded household and a gaggle of older brothers and sisters. He immediately became the center of attention in the household. Naturally, he was coddled and spoiled by his sisters, and Bill, Mike, and I saw him as another brother to play with. Pete enjoyed being the center of attention for almost three years before ceding his position as the baby of the family.

In the fall of 1958, Mother was once again pregnant with what would be Kelly number 10.

The Top Ten

(1959 - A 40'ish and very pregnant Emma Kelly sits at the piano at a night club with her four piece music combo. While they play, a patron and his wife approach the bandstand).

> *"Hey there boy! Tell me your favorite song?"*
> *"Emma, you look like you're about to pop. How many will this one make? Eight? Nine?"*
> *"Ten"*
> *"TEN!!! Holy Moly, Emma. How can anyone raise ten children and be out here playing the piano for geezers like us every night?"*
> *"Because playing for you every night helps pay for my children's food and clothes. And you've got a long way to go before you become a geezer." (looking at his wife). "Honey, what would you like to hear?"*
> *"Emma, can you play "Sentimental Journey?"*
> *"Absolutely! This is for you" (she breaks into "Sentimental Journey" and her band adjusts and follows suit).*

Not long after that dance, Mother found herself in the hospital giving birth to her 10th child.

With all of us crowding the waiting room at the Bulloch County Hospital, Doctor Waldo Floyd walked out of the delivery room smiling, and said to all of us, but Dad in particular....

"Well boys and girls, you have another sister! Congratulations George. You didn't get five boys to go with your five girls; but you definitely have your Top Ten."

On January 23rd, 1959, the birth of Patricia Lucille Kelly rounded out The Kelly Top Ten.

In the 1950's, the average family had 2 or 3 children. So a family of seven or eight children was unusual. A family of nine children was highly unusual. But ***TEN?*** Ten was a magical number.

Ten children was a story… a story that would make the newspapers and give regional notoriety to the large musical family from Statesboro. The story was not only about the family from South Georgia having ten children. It was also about the fact that all ten children were delivered by the same doctor.

Doctor Waldo Floyd was almost as much a member of the family as the six girls and four boys he had delivered. And he was just as much a part of the newspaper stories that followed the birth of George and Emma Kelly's tenth and final child.

Patricia Lucille Kelly, or 'Pat' as we would call her, was named for two people… another uncle, Pat Williams, and Lucille (Lucy) Purser Colosimo, a close friend and former band member of Mothers who had recently been killed in an automobile accident.

Pat's birthday will remain with all of us because that is the day we became known as "The Top 10"… "George and Emma Kelly's Top 10"… "Dr. Waldo Floyd's Top 10."

The story was yet another link in the chain that would connect the ten of us and keep us closely connected for the rest of our lives.

The age range between the ten of us spanned over twenty years. At the time of Pat's birth, Kitty, the oldest, was nearing graduation from nearby Georgia Southern University, which, at the time, was known as Georgia Teachers College. Phoebe, daughter #2, was in her sophomore year at the college. Jackie (#3) was in her senior year at Statesboro High School.

Paula was two years behind Jackie. I was two years behind Paula. Then Bill three years later, followed by Emaline, Mike and Pete, who was three at the time of Pat's birth.

We all lived at home, and given our age differences, we were engaged in very different levels of very different activities at the time. But we were the Top Ten. And we would be forever.

The Early Years

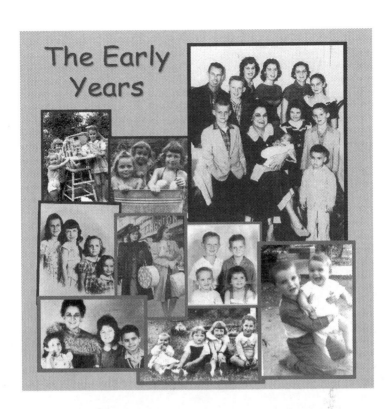

PART 2

Rules of the House

House Rules

The Kelly household was fast-paced, frenetic, in constant disarray, and always seemingly on the brink of chaos. In contrast to the frenzy of continuing motion and activities, however, the expectations that were placed on us, were seemingly simple and straightforward.

We were never given a specific set of rules that would govern our household or our lives, but they were there, and they were clearly understood by each of us. Rather than anything in writing, the rules came in the form of daily 'coachable moments', and in continually re-enforced messages that each of us heard throughout our lives growing up.

I'm sure if Mother or Dad were with us today, they would add other rules or expectations that were important to them, but the following are those that we seemed to hear most consistently and the ones we would hear about in no uncertain terms if we did not comply.

These were the mandates from Mother and Dad to each of us. And there was no question each was to be honored and carried out:

You will learn music....

Music was the centerpiece of our lives growing up together. That was in part due to Mother's profession, but also because of her very strong beliefs in the power of music. Just as she had been taught the value and the power of music from her mother, she intended to do the same with us.

Neither Mother nor Dad expected or tried to persuade us to be professional musicians or performers, but they certainly insisted that we learn and develop whatever musical talents we possessed.

That included learning to play instruments, learning to dance, and being comfortable performing on stage in front of audiences.

Having a family of ten children trained in the art of song and dance certainly had other benefits as well. What could be better than having a talented piano player? How about a talented piano player with her own traveling song and dance troupe? Mother learned early in her show business career that nothing could spice up an act like kids, and she just happened to have a group of attractive, talented singers and dancers that could put on quite a floorshow.

What began as *"Emma Kelly, the Piano Player"* became *"Emma Kelly and Family."*

At about age 4, each of us found ourselves in weekly tap dance and ballet classes. We literally learned to do the time step or the soft shoe, before we could read. By age 7 or 8, we were onstage somewhere doing song and dance routines as a family.

We all took music lessons of one form or another. Whether it was the piano, trumpet, saxophone, clarinet or trombone, we all learned an instrument. From Mother's perspective, it not only gave her more options as an entertainer, it would also benefit us later in our own lives.

Phoebe was the first family drummer in the "Emma Kelly Combo", until she graduated from college and moved away. Then I became the drummer. After I left, Emaline assumed the role... then Pat.

All of us danced. Depending on the venue, we performed song and dance routines to songs, such as *"Side by Side"*, or *"Consider Yourself at Home."*

In one way or another, we all were a part of the Emma Kelly Show. That included Daddy as well. He was the behind the scenes guy. He transported us from one venue to the next, helped with the sound system, delivered costumes, and whatever else may have been asked of him... usually at the last minute. On more than one occasion, that also meant getting up at 2:00 a.m. to come and rescue us from a broken down vehicle. Everyone contributed. From floorshows to dance recitals, to dance halls, Mother played the piano, the kids sang and danced, and Dad was behind the scenes, packing and unpacking, and taking care of all the loose ends.

Our dance training began for each of us at a very early age. Mother worked out an arrangement with the local dance studio in Statesboro in which she would play piano in exchange for us to take tap dance and ballet lessons. It so happened, however, that the 'local' studio was not local at all.

The *'Marilyn Yeomans School of Dance'* traveled to Statesboro from Savannah every week to conduct dance classes for students in the Statesboro and Bulloch County area. Each Wednesday, the large room at the Statesboro Recreation Department was converted into a make shift dance studio, where we took lessons, along with other students ranging in age from five to twenty-five. For Mother, that meant a steady Wednesday afternoon gig. For the ten of us, it meant that every Wednesday was 'tap dance and ballet lessons' day.

Tap dance and ballet lessons were not an unusual occurrence for girls. I think it is safe to say that the sisters enjoyed the experience. Tap dance lessons for adolescent boys were another matter.

The brothers were not exempt from tap dance and ballet lessons, and on many occasions, as teenagers, tap dance and ballet lessons conflicted with baseball practice or basketball practice or football practice, which also took place at the Recreation Center. That meant being pulled out of ball practice early, after being summoned by Mother in the presence of all of our team mates, to come inside for our tap dance and ballet lessons.

As is typical of community dance studios, most of the students in the weekly dance classes were female. In fact, other than the Kelly boys, ALL of the students were female, with one exception. The Marilyn Yeoman's School of Dance actually produced a male professional dancer from Statesboro. His name was Bee Carroll.

Bee was an exceptional talent, and went on to enjoy a very successful dance career in Las Vegas. So, there was one other exception to the dance classes being all-female. Bee's success notwithstanding, however, rest assured that no one was under the illusion that Bill, Mike, Pete or I would become the next Bee Carroll.

Each year, our tap dance and ballet lessons were concluded with the obligatory dance recital, performed in costumes and full make-up at the McCroan Auditorium at nearby Georgia Southern. If the weekly tap dance and ballet lessons weren't humiliating enough for the four boys, the recitals took the challenges of our struggling male adolescence to yet another level. Mother insisted that all of us, boys included, wear lipstick and rouge for our stage performances, all of which included dance routines with one or more female partners.

One of the more humbling dance recital experiences that Mike recalls as the pinnacle of his humiliation was a dance routine he performed with Emaline. Their duet was performed to the tune from the Broadway musical, *"South Pacific"* called *"I Enjoy Being a Girl."* They had rehearsed the routine in their Wednesday practices throughout the year, so he felt prepared to perform the dance at the annual recital. That was until he read the dance program. The entry on the program simply read:

"Mike and Emaline Kelly – "I Enjoy Being a Girl."

Though he appears to have recovered from this traumatic affront to what was at the time, a very fragile adolescent masculinity, he never quite had the same enthusiasm for tap dancing after reading that program.

Each of us brothers could list countless similar experiences, but our protestations fell on deaf ears. The humiliations of our tap dancing experiences did not stop or even slow down the Kelly song and dance machine. What began as weekly tap dance and ballet classes and annual dance recitals, eventually grew into what became known as the traveling dance troupe, simply known as *"The Kellys"*.

Mother knew she had an added attraction to offer her audiences, and she took full advantage. From the stages of American Legion halls, Elks Clubs, and Moose Lodges to outdoor venues on the back of a flatbed truck, *"The Kellys"* performed all over South Georgia.

Our performances were invariably accompanied by other students from our dance classes. There are many women in and around Bulloch County and southeast Georgia today, who were at one time or another, a part of the Emma Kelly Dance Show. Several of them went on to establish their own dance programs in Statesboro and elsewhere.

Looking back on our tap dancing days, we now know and appreciate the value of that experience. We know that the dance lessons were helpful as part of our social development, and we even know it helped us boys as athletes. We also know that those tap dance and ballet lessons and the many dance routines we performed as 'The Kellys', had as much to do as anything else in our lives, with keeping us close as a family.

Music in general and our dance routines in particular, gave us a common lifetime experience that we share to this day. So, whatever lessons there are to be learned about keeping families together and close throughout their lives, the Kellys would say, make dancing together part of the agenda.

You will Work!

Another common trait instilled in each of us early in life by both parents was the belief in the fundamental principle of work. Part of that edict was to instill the value and the principles of work in each of us, and part of it was to address the practical realities of what it took to support a family of ten children.

Dad worked seven days a week, many times late into the evening. In addition to her music, Mother took part-time jobs whenever and wherever she could find them. She worked with the Georgia State Patrol, issuing drivers licenses. She was a census worker, going house to house, counting heads, and reporting to the US Census Bureau. If it would supplement the families' finances, Mother and Dad did it.

We each found ways very early in life, to fend for ourselves and find ways to make our own money. For many families in the Statesboro area, we were 'Babysitting Central.' All of us, boys and girls alike babysat for many families in town, which provided a steady source of spending money for us. We worked in the school cafeteria and in other part-time jobs in school to pay for our school lunches and other school supplies. We had paper routes, worked in drug stores, department stores, the local recreation center, or the local tobacco markets… anyplace we could find a job and make money for ourselves, we found it, and we did it.

Having part-time jobs and making our own money was not just a way of life, it was a necessity. It lessened the financial burden of the family, and at the same time, it provided us the only means available to enjoy the basics of day-to-day life. The family never had a lot of money, but we did what we had to do to avoid *feeling* like we didn't have money.

Like music, entrepreneurship and a strong work ethic became defining characteristics for each of us. We believed that, rich or poor, you could make life what you wanted it to be... as long as you worked for it.

You Will Get an Education!

Like music and hard work, education was another of our golden rules.

I don't remember Mother or Dad saying, you will get a college degree, but there was no question that was what was expected of us, and probably even demanded. Georgia Southern was right next door, and it was a convenient and relatively inexpensive way for each of us to do just that.

Before college, though, we had to meet Mother's and Dad's expectations in grammar school and high school. In addition to the humiliation of Wednesdays being tap dance day, every six weeks, Wednesdays were also report card day, and some of us were not real enthusiastic about turning our report cards over to Mom and Dad for their review. The Bulloch County Board of Education viewed a 'C' as an acceptable grade. George and Emma Kelly felt otherwise. 'C's' on our report cards brought a lot of attention and discussion with Mom and Dad, and on those occasions when some of us brought home a report card with grades LESS than a C, the rest of the kids could take the evening off, because all of Mother and Dad's attention was devoted to that particular individual. The only sin worse than a C, D or F on our report card, was a C, D or F in conduct.

Probably the most divisive element amongst the ten of us in our entire childhoods was the division between those that looked forward to bringing their report cards home to Mother and Dad, and those that didn't. Surviving high school in the Kelly household seemed to make college a breeze. Amazingly, all ten of us received our college degrees… and four of the ten received advance degrees.

After graduating from high school, Kitty, then Phoebe, Jackie and Paula, proceeded directly to Georgia Southern. Kitty continued on to get her Master's Degree in Music, and Jackie continued to get her's in Education, leading to her teaching career.

Following high school, I proceeded to Georgia Southern just like my older sisters. The only difference was they went straight through to graduation, and I took the scenic route. Between stints at Georgia Southern, I went into the Air Force, and following my military obligation, I returned to Georgia Southern to finish my undergraduate work, then continued on to get my graduate degree at the University of Georgia.

Bill received a scholarship to play football at Georgia Tech, where he studied for three years before returning to Statesboro to finish his degree at Georgia Southern, and launch his real estate business.

Emaline followed her sisters going directly to Georgia Southern where she received her degree before joining Delta Airlines to become a flight attendant.

Mike received a scholarship to play football at Davidson College in North Carolina where he received his undergraduate degree, before continuing to get his law degree at Vanderbilt University.

Pete proceeded to Georgia Southern after finishing high school, and like me, he took his time. He got his degree on the seven year plan. Dad had the same comment for Pete that he did for me... *'He never let classes get in the way of his education.'*

Pat also took the indirect route to finishing her undergraduate work at Georgia Southern. Pat had extraordinary talent as a dancer, and had the opportunity to study dance in New York. That led to opportunities for her to perform in Broadway national tours with the likes of Dick Van Dyke and Donald O'Connor before returning to Georgia Southern to become the tenth Kelly to receive her college degree and the 9th to graduate from Georgia Southern.

The accomplishment of all ten of us earning college degrees was a major source of pride for both Mother and Dad, only to be topped by Mother, when later in life, she received an Honorary Doctorate degree from, where else, Georgia Southern University.

You Will Go to Church

Every Sunday morning, rain or shine, sleep or no sleep, sick or well, tired or not, we got into the biggest car that Mom and Dad could afford at the time, and made our way to the First Baptist Church for Sunday School and Church services.

Many times when I was Mother's drummer, we would get in at 2:00 or 3:00 o'clock on a Saturday night, from performing, and think, "Surely, we will be able to sleep in and not have to go to Sunday school tomorrow morning."

Never happened!

No matter the circumstance, at seven a.m. on Sunday mornings, we were rousted out of bed, and herded into the hectic ritual of baths, showers, and finding something suitable to wear to church, and out the door by 9:30. As we paraded out to the car, Mother would be at the door with a wet wash cloth in hand, to make sure our clothes were presentable, and our faces and hands were clean. If we happened to miss a spot, she and that wet wash cloth would find it and remove it, along with any skin that may have been in the vicinity.

Neither Mother nor Dad would be characterized as being overly 'religious', but their faith (especially Mother) was unwavering. Mother's commitment to being at Sunday school and church services, where she played piano for Sunday school, was as certain as the sunrise. That included Vacation Bible School during the summers, Sunday evening services, youth services, and anything else that the Church may have sponsored. The First Baptist Church was as much a part of our lives growing up, as was school, the Recreation Center, or tap dance lessons.

Mother played piano for her Sunday School class and sang in the Church choir, which afforded her yet another way to watch over her own flock. Positioned strategically in the choir behind the preacher's pulpit, she was in a perfect position to monitor our behavior during the church service. She would (1) confirm that we were present in the congregation; (2) confirm that we were paying attention; and, (3) ensure that we were not misbehaving in any way. Should any one of those three expectations be violated, we would be in for some serious coaching and counseling when we got home.

One Sunday after Sunday School, a friend of mine and I decided to skip the church service and hang out in the Howard Johnsons restaurant which was across the street. We timed our stay to be on the church steps when the service was over, to ensure that we would blend in with the crowd as everyone exited the church. Along with my brothers and sisters, I made my way to the car and we proceeded home, as if nothing out of the ordinary had happened. When home, as she was preparing Sunday dinner, Mother casually asked me what I thought of the service. Trying my best to fake it, I told her I thought it was a good service. Each of her questions took me a little further down the trail of being busted, at which point the conversation and subsequent actions took a very different tone.

Whatever God's punishment may have been for skipping church, it would not have been as severe as Mother's. I think that was the last time I skipped church, and I probably served as a deterrent for any of my brothers and sisters who may have considered it.

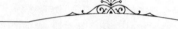

You will take care of your brothers and sisters....

Given the challenge of managing a household with ten children and both parents working six and seven days a week, much of the family parenting and day to day household duties were assumed by the older sisters. A natural order seemed to emerge in which each of them seemed to concentrate on certain ones of the rest of us, as if they were our adoptive second parent. Whatever else they had going on in their own lives in their efforts to be normal teenagers, much of their time was devoted to looking after the rest of us. As the family grew even larger, that routine became an ingrained part of the family culture... *you take care of your brothers and sisters.*

Perhaps again due to our numbers and our limited resources, we discovered early that we were stronger as a group than any of us were as individuals, and that proved itself out over and over again.

We lived the credo, *'the power of the wolf is in the pack!'*

From the times in our childhoods when one needed a little extra money, to the times in our earlier adult lives when one brother or sister lived with another, to the times today when one is in need, the others unfailingly step up to help out.

You will behave!!!

One of the most common and repeated phrases to come from both Mother and Dad was, *"You may not be smart, but you can always behave!"* (At least, that's what they said to me).

In school, we were all expected to get good grades, and we got considerable 'coaching' when we did not. Many times, it seemed that the grade that Mom and Dad paid the most attention to was 'Conduct.' A bad grade in 'Conduct' carried far greater consequences than a bad grade in Algebra.

Outside of school, the standards were even higher. Mother was a public figure, and she was very careful as to how she presented herself to her public. She considered us an extension of her public persona and we were held to the same standards she held for herself. Whether in the public spotlight, or in a casual conversation, we were taught in very clear terms how we were to conduct ourselves. From our posture, to our demeanor, to our language, to our actions, the expectations were clear. Pay attention to people you are conversing with. Look them directly in the eye. Stand up straight. Do not slouch. Enunciate clearly. Be polite, considerate and respectful.

Dad's expectations were no different, but his approach came from a different perspective. His was a more simplistic, overarching view of right and wrong. Show business or no show business; public figure or private individual; talking to the boss or the janitor; whether in a crowd of people or whether no one is watching, there is a right way to behave, and a wrong way to behave. And we had better be behaving the right way.

His values were shaped more by the basic principles and honor among men. If you say you're going to do something, do it. And don't do it halfway. Do what's right. Tell the truth.

In Dad's eyes, we didn't need a lot of rules. Right and wrong was a matter of common sense, and we were expected to behave accordingly.

In short, there was an unwritten but well understood code of how we were to conduct ourselves, in public or in private… and with the exception of a few occasional lapses, we adhered pretty well to that code.

You Will Speak Proper English!

Nothing seemed to grate on Mother more than hearing someone butcher the English language. Whether it was poor grammar, improper subject-verb conjugation, poor vocabulary, poor diction or elocution, a dangling participle, slurring of words or cursing, she shuddered when she heard the King's English misused in any way, and she let it be known.

She was taught the value of speaking and writing properly by her mother, and she was determined to teach us the same. She felt anything less was not only a sign of ignorance, but also a poor reflection on us as individuals and on the family.

She was a regular subscriber to the Reader's Digest, and more than the stories included in each edition, she enjoyed the vocabulary quizzes or the 'word of the day' that accompanied each edition. We were quickly corrected anytime our language did not meet the standards of proper English, and we were frequently quizzed on vocabulary, subject-verb agreement, verb conjugations, and other forms of proper use of the language.

Mother's reactions to improper speech were comparable to her reaction if we skipped church or missed a dance lesson or made a "C" in Conduct. To say, "o'er der" instead of "over there" would lead to a series of drills to properly enunciate our 'th's'. The same would occur with the dangling participle such as "Where are you at?" Those were examples of what she described as lazy speech, just as she felt cursing, in addition to being crude and inappropriate, was a form of laziness.

A failure to properly pronounce words evoked the same reaction... "Runnin'", as opposed to "Running." "Imona go," as opposed to "I'm going to go." "I dunno," as opposed to "I don't know." Any of these faux pas spoken in her presence, along with any other forms of butchering of the English language would result in an on-the-spot mini lesson, accompanied by repeated drills until she was satisfied the error was out of our system.

Mother's training as a child, combined with her sensitivity of how we presented ourselves in public made her a stickler for how we communicated, verbally and written. And for the most part, any grammatical errors in this publication notwithstanding, we got it!

We Do What We Have to Do

Given our size, our pace and our lack of resources, we seldom had the luxury of crying over spilled milk.

If you made a mistake… fix it and move on. If you fell and hurt yourself… rub it hard, get up, and move on. If you felt bad about something… correct it, put it behind you and move on.

We simply didn't have the time or circumstances to bemoan our setbacks, and given the numbers, we had ample opportunities for setbacks. We were a large family in constant motion which created multiple opportunities for mishaps, accidents and near tragedies. Miraculously, we not only survived them, we seemed to grow stronger and more resolute with each one. The unspoken rule was when there are accidents, mishaps, or setbacks, you come together as a family, take care of the problem, move on, and don't look back.

One of the rare occasions when I saw Mother cry was when she learned that a very close friend of hers had died. It was a Saturday morning when she received the phone call. Completely distraught, she stayed in her bedroom all morning long and into the afternoon. She had a performance engagement to deliver that Saturday night and, given her emotional state, I was convinced she would have to cancel.

About three o'clock that afternoon, she came out of her room, fully dressed and made up for the evening performance, and said, 'We've got to get moving. We've got a show to do.'

I was stunned. It was if nothing had happened.

Looking back on it now, I know she was grieving and carried her grief into her Saturday night performance and beyond. She simply didn't have the luxury of allowing her grief to prevent her from going on with the show. That too, was a fundamental belief that began with Mother and Dad, and filtered down to each of us. No matter the odds, no matter the circumstance, working together, obstacles can and will be overcome. The show must go on.

The fire that destroyed our house and everything we owned, the many illnesses, incidents, and accidents that occurred with each of us, and the financial hardships we endured were all defining moments that shaped that attitude....

'You take the cards you're dealt, do what you have to do, and move on.'

All the lessons we learned from Mother and Dad were lessons that were reaffirmed by our friends and neighbors in the community. We heard the same messages in Church and in school that we heard at home. We heard the same messages from our teachers and coaches that we heard from our parents. The town of Statesboro, with its small town atmosphere, strong sense of community and its affiliation with a growing college, served as the perfect complement and backdrop to our story and helped to reinforce these and other lessons firmly within us.

PART 3

Growing Up

Home Sweet Home

Statesboro, Georgia is nestled in the southeast corner of the state, where some of the most fertile farmlands in the country converge with the sandy bottom low country of coastal Georgia and South Carolina. The area annually produces rich harvests of peanuts, tobacco, cotton, and soybeans, yet it serves as a gateway to the low country and coastal beaches from Savannah to Hilton Head, down to the Golden Isles of Georgia.

In the 1960's the town's rich culture of agriculture seemed to comfortably co-exist with the college town environment provided by Georgia Southern College. Mud covered overalls were interchangeable with madras shirts and seersucker blazers. Pick-up trucks and tractors shared parking lots with sports cars and sedans. Tobacco auctions and farmers markets by day led to Country Club socials by night. They all had a place at the table in Statesboro.

We enjoyed the small town qualities of Mayberry RFD, the excitement and cultural advantages of a college town, and the friendships of hardworking people who loved their community and came together in times of need. Our lives were shaped and influenced largely by our parents, but the community of Statesboro also made an indelible mark on each one of us. What we have become or have attained in life as a family, would not have been realized were it not for the friends, family, and community leaders of our hometown.

Every town or community has its social hierarchy, and the Statesboro community in the 1960's was no different. It can safely be said that the Kelly family was not amongst the top tier of that hierarchy, either financially or socially. But there was never a time in which we did not feel universally accepted and supported by the community, from the town elites, to everyone else in and around the town.

Statesboro was a much simpler place when we were growing up. The after school hangout was the College Pharmacy with its classic soda fountain that was commonplace in those days. All major shopping took place downtown in stores like Minkovitz Department Store, Tilli's, Rosenberg's, or Men and Boys Store. We did our food shopping at the Piggly Wiggly or at Otis's Superette.

The hardware store was Buggy and Wagon. The breakfast spot was the Nic-Nac Grill. The late night gathering place was Franklin's Restaurant, which was the only 24 hour restaurant in town. The other main restaurants in town were The Paragon and Mrs. Bryant's Kitchen.

At the time, US Highway 301, which flowed through the middle of town, was the major north-south thoroughfare from New England and New York to Florida. The Statesboro economy relied heavily on the steady stream of tourists as they drove to Florida from their homes in the northeast. Statesboro hotels and restaurants, such as the Crossroads Motel, Bryant's Motel, The Paragon, and Mrs. Bryant's Kitchen catered as much to the tourists as they did the local population and provided another source of part-time jobs for us growing up.

The Interstate highway system changed everything. I-95 became the new north-south route to Florida, and US 301 went the way of Route 66 and all the other now 'historic' roads around the country. The hotels, restaurants and other tourist related businesses from Maine to Florida that relied on US 301 traffic were dramatically affected, including those in Statesboro. As the stream of tourists shifted from Highway 301 to I-95, many of the businesses that relied on those tourists also went the way of Route 66 soon after.

As the Statesboro economy adjusted and continued to prosper, the one constant, and perhaps cornerstone of our youth, was the Recreation Center.

Max Lockwood and the Statesboro Recreation Department had an enormous impact on our lives. It seemed there was always something going on at the Recreation Center that kept us off the streets, taught us skills, and taught us how to be good citizens.

We learned basketball, football and baseball at the Recreation Center. We learned to swim at the Recreation Center. We learned to play tennis at the Recreation Center. We took tap dance and ballet lessons at the Recreation Center. We attended sock hops at the Recreation Center. In short, we grew up and learned how to be good citizens at the Recreation Center.

Whatever the sport season, the Recreation Center had organized programs. From Midget football, to Little League and American Legion baseball, to men's softball leagues, to basketball leagues, we learned the basic skills and sportsmanship of all sports.

'Tween Teens' was an organization for pre-teens and adolescents which sponsored sock hops, concerts and dance lessons. The Happy Go Lucky Club (or HGL's), provided teen-aged girls a place to be and a place to learn the skills and social graces of becoming a woman.

Saturday mornings were a time for marble tournaments, cartoons, 'Little Rascal' re-runs and hot dog lunches. The Pavalon (named for the butchered pronunciation of 'pavilion') was located next to the swimming pool, and was the site for concerts, dances and other social events. You could almost always find us at 'The Pavalon' on Friday nights, especially in the summertime.

All of this was provided under the tutelage and leadership of Max Lockwood. The Recreation Center was our home away from home, and Max was our surrogate father. He wanted us to learn sports, but more importantly he wanted us to learn sportsmanship and citizenship. He was happy for us to be good athletes, as long as, in the process, we became good citizens. There was no circumstance, no occasion, and no situational need that the Statesboro Recreation Center did not address, and we took full advantage.

The First Baptist Church in Statesboro also was a foundation for us. We were there seemingly as often as we were at the Recreation Center. Every Sunday morning, we attended Sunday school and Church. During the summers, we attended Vacation Bible School, and every other function hosted or sponsored by the Church. Mother played piano for her Sunday school classes and sang in the Church choir, most of the time, after being out all night playing for a dance the Saturday night before.

The business community of Statesboro was supportive of Dad's sign painting business. There was not a store or business in town that had not used Dad for their signs or advertising. He was a master craftsman and artist. He worked tirelessly, and the local business community called on him regularly.

The business community also was an invaluable and reliable source for part-time jobs for the kids. Part-time jobs were essential to the finances of the Kelly household as well as being the lifeblood of any discretionary spending we might enjoy. We always looked to the local business owners in town for work, and more often than not, they were willing to hire us.

Similarly, Mother was called upon by almost every family in town at one time or another to play for weddings, anniversary parties, school plays, church socials, or other events. In between, she provided entertainment for the Lions Club, the Rotary Club, the Kiwanis Club, the Country Club and a host of other events that looked to her for entertainment.

School was obviously central to our lives growing up, and our teachers and coaches were another major influence. All of us remember with fondness those teachers and coaches that helped guide and encourage us. The boys especially remember Coach Ernest Teel, Coach Ray Williams, and many others that taught us, disciplined us, and shaped us.

As the Statesboro community helped prepare us to become adults and good citizens, Georgia Southern was right there to help put some of the polishing touches on our development. In our earliest years, Georgia Teachers College was just beginning its transition to become Georgia Southern University. The proximity and access to Georgia Southern was pivotal in our education and development, and it can be argued that we would not have had the success in all of us getting college degrees, were Georgia Southern not located in the town where we grew up.

In addition to providing us convenient access to a college diploma, Georgia Southern also offered an added cultural dimension to our development that can only be experienced in a university setting. From guest lectures, to fine arts exhibits, to rock concerts, Georgia Southern provided us access to programs and events that only added to our cultural development.

From Kitty the oldest to Pat the youngest, the ten of us spanned over twenty years in age difference. That meant that most every family in Statesboro in the 1950's, 60's and early '70's had one or more children that was a classmate of a Kelly. Through our classmates and friends, we touched a lot of families, and those families touched us. We were welcomed guests for parties, sleepovers, and other activities that gave us access and visibility to how other families lived, and we grew from those experiences and friendships that live on today. Every class reunion or chance encounter with old classmates and friends brings back a flood of memories of a glorious time, in a glorious place that we had the privilege of calling home... Statesboro, Georgia.

Today, though most of us have moved elsewhere, Statesboro remains the foundation of our childhood and the foundation of our family. Today, we get to enjoy our childhood and family memories in a completely different, but equally satisfying way... through the Averitt Arts Center and The Emma Kelly Theater.

The building that was once the bank where Mother and Dad did their banking is now home to the Averitt Center for the Arts, and the adjacent building that was once the Georgia Theater, where we went to the movies every Saturday, is now the home of the Emma Kelly Theater.

The activities associated with the Averitt Center and the Emma Kelly Theater, provide us opportunities to return home and reflect on our childhoods and our family. For some of us, it has also provided us the opportunity to perform on the stage that now bears Mother's name.

The small farming community that helped Mother and Dad through some of the biggest challenges in their lives, and helped raise the ten of us, and helped keep us on the straight and narrow in our own development, is now a growing, prosperous, and sophisticated city. It was our home then; it remains our home away from home today, forever linked to the very core of our lives.

Going With the Flow

After Pat's birth, life progressed swiftly for the Top Ten.

The older girls were performing regularly and an integral part of Mother's shows. The boys had become regulars at the local Recreation Center, and the younger brothers and sisters began to ease themselves into the day-to-day rhythm and routines of the family.

As the older sisters moved from high school into college, and into their own lives as adults, the younger siblings were being trained to step in and take their place. Mother had created her own farm system to fill the talent void as her family grew up and out.

Dad's business remained steady, as did his love of flying. Working seven days a week seemed to be the only way to stay up with the demands of the family, but he never seemed to complain. Sunday afternoons at the Statesboro Airport continued to be his major source of recreation and diversion from those demands.

The boys loved sports. When not taking tap dance lessons or helping with Dad's business, we could be found at the Statesboro Recreation Center playing baseball, basketball, football or any other competitive activity that the center offered. We had the same passion for athletics that we had for music.

In appearance, the ten of us were as different as we were alike. Our personalities and attitudes, however, were cut from the same cloth. We were all trained in the art of social interaction just as we had been trained in music. We were taught how to engage our audiences off stage, just as we did onstage. The combination of our genetics, our musical training and our social training prepared us with engaging and outgoing personalities, and conditioned us to reach out to anyone, young or old, rich or poor, in conversation. Like Mother and Dad, we never met a stranger.

The more we grew, however, the more complex our household became. There were more moving parts, going in more different directions. At the same time, when Mother's performances were becoming more and more frequent, demanding more of the children's time, the older sisters were becoming more independent and more engaged in their own activities. The juggling act of school, dating, social events and part-time jobs competed with their responsibilities as family caretakers and as performers. The boys were becoming as active in athletics as they were in music. Football, basketball, and baseball games began to conflict with tap dance lessons, floor shows and dance recitals. Each year, as we grew older, the art of balancing family responsibilities with our individual activities and interests became more challenging and more frenzied.

Within the chaos, though, there seemed to be an inexplicable calm. There was a method to the madness that was unspoken, but clearly understood by each of us. It had become our normal.

"Where Are My Socks?"

(Mother, to my brother Mike on a Sunday morning while getting ready for Church)….

"Mike, Pete is going to wear your suit. It's getting too small for you, and he needs to start wearing a suit to church."
"What am I going to wear?"
"You wear Bill's suit."
"BILL's suit. I can't wear Bill's suit. It's too big."
"It will work. Here, try it on."
*(Bill walks in) "Hey that's **my** suit!"*
"Mike's going to wear your suit."
"That's too big for him. And what will I wear?"
"You wear Ross' suit."
"Mamma, I can't wear Ross' suit. It's too big for me. Plus, it has that light bulb burn on the arm."
"It will work. And no one will notice that burn on the arm."
"What's Ross going to wear?"
"He's going to wear Daddy's suit."
"DADDY's suit! (laughing) That's way too big for him. He can't wear that."
"Hush and put on these pants."

Saying that our experience growing up Kelly was an adventure would be an understatement. Everything was in constant motion, everything was in volume, and everything was communal. There were no individual possessions that were not subject to being confiscated or reissued to someone else if the circumstance warranted.

To add to the fun, on many days there were more than ten of us. Our house seemed to be a magnet for many of our friends. Sometimes, it was hard to differentiate one of the Kelly children from one of our friends or neighbors. With so many moving parts, it was hard to tell who was who, sometimes even for Mother or Dad.

Billy Cook was our next door neighbor, and as an only child, he spent as much time at our house as he did his own. He was in the age range of Emaline and Mike and was like an eleventh Kelly. When preparing for a performance, Mother had a habit of having one of us help fasten her bra or zip her dress when in the final stages of dressing. Whether it was one of us, Billy Cook, or some other friend that happened to be in the vicinity, whoever was closest at the time got the request for assistance. Some of our unsuspecting friends may have been unprepared for this task, but for regulars like Billy, that was just another routine activity in the Kelly household.

Had we been a government, we would have been characterized as a socialist dictatorship, with two benevolent dictators at the helm. With ten children and limited funds, Mother and Dad learned quickly, and taught each of us, to conserve and consolidate in any way that would keep us fed, clothed, and housed.

We had a 'sock box', which was a large cardboard box that all socks were placed. So all of us, boys and girls alike, took whatever socks were available for whatever the occasion. In our earlier years, that was somewhat easy, as everyone wore white socks, and we never paid attention to whether they were girls 'bobby socks' or boys athletic socks. If they were white, they worked. Fit was not an issue... too big, too small, no matter. If we could get them on our feet, we wore them, and we were never too proud or too uncomfortable to fold the toes underneath our feet inside the shoes.

Similarly, we had a 'shoe bag', which served the same purpose. Sunday dress shoes, athletic shoes, high heels, tennis shoes, saddle oxfords, and Bass Weejun penny loafers all could be found in the shoe bag. All were put to use on a first come, first serve basis. For the most part, we could make a distinction between girls' shoes and boys' shoes, although, the older girls black and white or brown and white 'saddle shoes' easily went both ways. There were multiple occasions when Mother or Dad had to referee arguments between one of the sisters and one of the brothers, both laying claim to a pair of girls' saddle oxfords.

The shoe bag, however, was not to be confused with the '**TAP** shoe bag.' The tap shoe bag contained tap shoes, ballet shoes, toe shoes and other dancing accessories devoted to our stage performances, and remained largely in Mother's control. It was a staple for our dance lessons and our shows, but was also convenient for Mother on unannounced or spontaneous performances when someone might request a song and dance routine. Mother never missed an opportunity to show off her children's tap dancing talents, and in many cases, the direction came on a moment's notice with neither us nor the audience receiving any advance warning. That type of moment could occur at a Rotary Club luncheon, a family gathering, or if one or more of us happened to visit her at one of her solo performances. Our typical response on those occasions was to say we, '*We would love to, but we don't have our shoes with us.*' We were always taught to be polite. But we were also taught, 'When someone asks you to perform, you perform!'

Mother made sure that our tap shoes were always available and that the absence of the appropriate shoes could never be used as an excuse not to perform. We would invariably have to dig into the tap shoe bag, and hopefully find a pair of shoes that fit.

Practicality and innovation were essential attributes when it came to raising ten children with limited resources. That said, Mother and Dad were nothing, if not practical and innovative when it came to doing more with less. Just like our shoes and socks, all clothing was community clothing, and hand-me-downs were never frowned upon. Getting 'new' clothes did not always mean 'NEW.' Regardless of the source or the degree of wear, if you wore it for the first time, it was considered by us to be new! Cast-off clothes from other families, whose children had outgrown them, were even better, and we wore them proudly.

Meals were also a creative endeavor. Mother did not always cook, but she certainly had mastered the art of cooking in volume. Her meals were tasteful and well-seasoned (we now believe to disguise some of the ingredients), but her main emphasis was on how to make a little go a long way.

Stews were a staple. They typically included any and everything that could be found in the cabinets or in the refrigerator, and anything not eaten today, would certainly appear on our plates tomorrow. There were many occasions when left-over stew from the night before turned into a breakfast dish the next morning, which, if the only option available, looked pretty good.

Mother was also a most creative bargain hunter. Long before there was a Costco, Sam's, or Walmart, Mother knew every low budget, second hand, and consignment store owner in south Georgia, on a first name basis. And they loved to see her coming.

When she bought, she bought in bulk. It was not an uncommon occurrence to see mother arrive home with large boxes or crates of clothing, trinkets, food, or other items that were a bargain find for her that day. She brought home food that had a shelf life measured in years. She brought home clothes that did not fit anyone in the family. Her rationale was, *'Someday, someone will be able to wear this.'*

Once she brought home a crate of brass ash trays, shaped in the form of a large (bigger than your hand) housefly. When we all asked in amazement "What in the world are these things?" She simply said, "They will make nice gifts for someone someday."

I suppose this would be the appropriate time for the housefly gift disclaimer.... Which is to acknowledge to anyone reading this, who may have, at some point, received a large, brass housefly ashtray for Christmas or your birthday or anniversary from any of the Kellys, that as unique and unusual as that gift may have appeared to be, it was one of more than fifty that were purchased by Mother and given as gifts.

Perhaps from the same store, Mother found a similar brass ashtray that was shaped in the form of a large crab. Another time she came home with a box of glass snow globes that I'm certain wound up under many Christmas trees as gifts from the family.

Mother and Dad were equally pragmatic when it came to finances.

Seven day workweeks were common for Dad and his sign painting business. His shop was located behind what is now the Averitt Center and Emma Kelly Theater, and you could usually find him there six and seven days a week.

Long before mother made a living playing the piano full-time, she took any odd job that would augment the coffers. She was a contract employee with the Bureau of the Census, hired to go door-to-door to take the census every ten years. She always volunteered to go into the less affluent areas of town and for very pragmatic reasons.

First, she knew many of the census workers would not be interested in those areas, which would always assure her of getting an assignment. Second, she was paid by the headcount, and she knew she would be more likely to get more heads, and more dollars, by working those neighborhoods.

She loved to tell the story of an occasion during the 1960 census, when she took 4 year old Pete with her as she went from door to door in one of the black neighborhoods in town. As Mother conducted her interviews with the family inside the house, Pete played with the other children outside. At the conclusion of the interview, Mother came out and jokingly took the hand of one of the black children and said, "Come on Pete, let's go." Pete frantically tried to intercept her and proclaimed, *"Mother, I'M Pete. I'M Pete."*

She was a notary public. Again her rationale was, it wasn't much, but every $1 or $2 fee for notary signatures and stamps helped. She distributed promotional fliers announcing new businesses or sales promotions for local businesses in the community. She worked for the Georgia State Patrol issuing and renewing driver's licenses. Every week, she occupied a small card table in the hallway of the courthouse, where she served as the administrative arm of the State Patrol, filling out the paperwork for new and expired licenses.

(Emma, in the hallway of the courthouse sitting at a cardboard table; issuing driver's licenses. Newborn infant, Pat, is in a baby seat on the floor by her side. Man in his mid-late 70's approaches to get his license renewed)

> *"Well Earl, look at you! How are you doing?"*
> *"I'm doing fine, Emma. I see you've got a new addition to the family. I saw your picture in the paper. Miriam cut it out, and is showing everybody that comes over. She's telling everyone 'This is the woman that's going to play for our 60th wedding anniversary.' You still up for it?"*
> *"I wouldn't miss it for the world…Sunday afternoon in the Church Social Room."*
> *"Emma, I'm supposed to get my license renewed. But they say I'm supposed to take a driver's test before they'll give it to me."*
> *"Earl, can you still see alright? If you can, we can take care of that."*
> *Smiling, "I can see you and that pretty baby!"*
> *"Well, alright! I think you just got your license renewed."*

Getting a driver's license is a big rite of passage for most teenagers, and it certainly was for each of us. On my 16th birthday, when I was eligible to get my driver's license, I did so with a classmate, Ed Mikell, whose birthday was a day before mine. We were both prepared to go directly to the courthouse after school and complete the exam, knowing Mother was there to coach us through whatever issues we might encounter in the process. Notwithstanding a morning rain, that could have delayed our driver's test, we were both issued our licenses, with an official stamp that said,

> *"Authorized by the Georgia State Patrol.*
> *Issued by Emma Kelly, Notary Public."*

Beyond the ten of us and Ed Mikell, there were many people in Bulloch County who received learner's permits and driver's licenses with the same stamp. Just another way for Mother to make ends meet.

Mother and Dad also made ample use of the concept of bartering with local merchants and businesses in the community, which enabled us to enjoy many activities growing up that we might not otherwise have enjoyed. Dad painted signs for the local movie theaters (Remember the Georgia and State Theaters, and the Drive-In Movie Theater?). He painted the posters that announced coming attractions, in exchange for movie passes for each of us. We were able to go to the movies anytime for free; and no one took more advantage of that deal than Mother. He did the same for the Recreation Department, in exchange for free passes to the swimming pool and free swimming lessons. Mother played piano for the local dance studio in exchange for free tap dance and ballet lessons for each of us. She did the same for music lessons and musical instruments.

Life was hectic, chaotic, disorganized and sometimes barely survivable. Through it all, however, we not only survived, but seemed to prosper. We were living evidence of the phrase, *'Necessity is the mother of invention.'*

Mother and Dad found ways to make it work, when conventional wisdom suggested it would not. Living through those times together and learning to adapt and evolve to the conditions presented to us, further instilled in us a sense of togetherness and a belief that any obstacle or challenge could be overcome. We had no choice but to get through the day, and the only way we could, was by working together. We had no choice but to be flexible and innovative. We had no choice but to rely on our parents, ourselves, and our brothers and sisters. As a result, we developed a deeply rooted confidence and belief that, with creativity and flexibility, you can make anything work.

That applied to our road shows as well.

Emma's Traveling Musical Show

"Hey, look outside. We got a new car."
"We did? What did we get?"
"A Lincoln Continental."
"A Lincoln Continental?"
"Yep. Its eight years old, but it can hold just about all of us, and all the drums and musical equipment can fit in the trunk."

Mother learned early that if she had any chance of making ends meet playing the piano, she had to go wherever the music took her. She also learned that her audiences not only enjoyed her, but enjoyed her children's song and dance routines as well. Mother continued to perform as a solo artist, but more and more her performances were becoming a family affair. We were the South Georgia version of the Bob Hope shows that traveled to foreign outposts such as Korea and Viet Nam. Our travels took us to every small town and city in South Georgia and beyond, and when she brought the kids along for added entertainment value that was when the fun usually began. Our traveling vaudeville act covered all of Georgia, and parts of Florida and South Carolina.

The phrase, 'herding cats' could easily be applied to us trying to get organized and mobilized for a road trip.

"Is everyone in the car? Where's Jackie? Did each of you pack your costumes?"
"Jackie's still cleaning up the kitchen."
"I have the 'sailor suit' outfit. I'm assuming that's what we are doing."

> *"I didn't bring the sailor suit outfit. I brought the Hula dance outfit."*
> *"We are doing both numbers, so you need both outfits. Go get both outfits, and tell Jackie to leave the kitchen and get in the car."*
> *"Well, hang on. I've got to get my sailor suit costume."*
> *"Get my hula costume while you are in there."*
> *"Did you bring my shoes?"*
> *"Mama, the kitchen is a mess. Are you just going to leave it like that?"*
> *"I didn't bring your shoes. I didn't know I was supposed to bring your shoes."*
> *"It is 4:30, and we have to be there by 6:00. And it's a two hour drive."*
> *"I don't know why we have to do both numbers."*
> *"Because that's what we're doing! Why is taking Pat so long?"*

Getting on the road was only the start of the adventure. In the 1960's, even brand new cars were not as reliable as cars today, and we very seldom had a new car. Our cars were generally used and the bigger the better. Mother and Dad's car buying criteria consisted of (1) how many people can physically fit in the front and back seats without being stopped by the police? And (2) how many musical instruments can we fit in the trunk? Reliability was always trumped by affordability and space. So, anytime we traveled more than fifty miles, road trips were an adventure.

Getting to the venue was generally not the challenge. Cars always perform well in broad daylight, when garages are open and plenty of help can be found. It is when you are driving home at 11:00 o'clock at night, when all the stations are closed, and your miles from the nearest form of life, that the fun would usually begin. Sometimes, it was as simple as running out of gas.

> *"I thought you said you got gas!"*
> *"I said we SHOULD get gas!"*

Sometimes it was a leaking radiator, a flat tire, or something more serious, like a blown engine. It didn't happen always, but when it did, it always happened at night…on a rural road…miles from the nearest farm house or gas station…at a time when no one was on the road except the Emma Kelly Traveling Road Show.

There were other times, when it wasn't the car's fault or even the driver's. On more than one occasion, it was an innocent deer in the middle of the road who suffered the misfortune of not knowing the Kellys were on the road that night. We saw, firsthand, the phrase, '*deer in the headlights.*'

A conservative accounting over the years was:

Kellys – 11
Deer – 0

No matter the cause, no matter the predicament, on each of those occasions, our rescuer ultimately was Dad. There were no cell phones. There was no 911 and no 24 hour roadside assistance. The call invariably came from a local farmhouse or the nearest phone booth which was usually miles away. Thank God, Dad was always home and usually coherent enough to get the call. We learned later that he had developed the habit of sleeping with one ear listening for the phone, until everyone was home, safe and sound.

Looking back, none of us know or can remember how we managed those situations. How long did it take us to find a phone? How long did it take Dad to dress and get on the road? How did he *find* us? Only Dad would have known how many times he went out into the night, generally past midnight, to retrieve us from a broken down car. But he always did.

When the car wasn't broken down, it was usually exceeding the speed limit. Even then, the Kellys had developed a reputation with the Georgia State Patrol. Driving on the desolate back roads of South Georgia at two o'clock in the morning, it was easy to assume that we were the only car on the road. So, exceeding the speed limit didn't seem to be a big deal.

Most of the time, when we were stopped for speeding, we generally had six, seven, or eight people in the car, and we always had a good story. Sometimes we got a break, when the trooper was sympathetic to our cause, and sometimes, whatever money we made from our performances went to paying speeding tickets.

Those days served as a preamble to the notoriety Mother would later receive with the Georgia State Patrol for having a heavy foot on I-16 driving back and forth from Savannah to Statesboro late at night. Those driving habits were finely honed years earlier, with the Emma Kelly Traveling Musical Extravaganza.

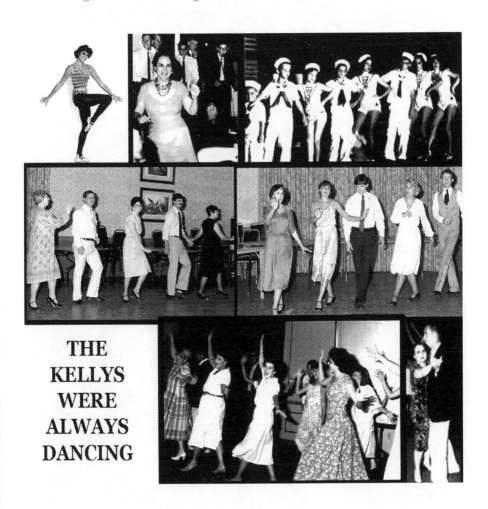

THE KELLYS WERE ALWAYS DANCING

Mother Entertains the President

By the 1960's, Fort Stewart had become an increasingly strategic installation for the US military. World War II and the Korean War had ended, but the Cold War was now in full swing. Fort Stewart served as a training ground for troops being deployed to NATO bases in and around Europe and the emerging conflict in Viet Nam.

The installation became even more vital in late 1962 when, at the height of the cold war, the US discovered nuclear weapons on the island of Cuba. It was learned that the weapons belonged to the Soviet Union. That discovery set the stage for what became known as the Cuban missile crisis. In a matter of hours after the discovery of the missiles, the US military went on full alert. The National Guard was activated, and thousands of troops were mobilized to prepare for a potential was with Cuba and the Soviet Union. Given its location and support infrastructure, Ft. Stewart became a major staging area for potential troop deployments to Cuba, should that be necessary.

As the country watched and waited to see if we were going to war, thousands of soldiers were quietly being dispatched to Ft. Stewart in preparation for that possibility. The base did not have the housing to accommodate the massive influx of troops, but it did have over 5,000 square miles of swamp land, that would provide the perfect location for what the military called a 'bivouac', or a massive tent city. As thousands of soldiers and national guardsmen suddenly found themselves miles from home and living in tents in the South Georgia swamp, the USO went into action. They called on their favorite entertainer. Mother then went into action and mobilized her own troops.

Armed with musicians and tap dancers, the Emma Kelly Show made its way into the swamps, and on the back of flatbed trailers, entertained the troops. She and her troupe did not have the fame or notoriety of Bob Hope and his entourage, but they had the same passion and delivered everything the USO had asked for and more. She did several performances both in the fields and on the base over the course of the crisis, and one of those happened to have a VIP in attendance.

On November 26, 1962, President Kennedy himself visited the base to inspect the facilities and visit with the troops that had been bivouacked out in the fields. During his visit, the President was treated to a dinner and entertainment at the base Officer's Club. One of the entertainers was none other than our Miss Emma.

She only performed two songs while the President was there, but they were two songs she would remember for the rest of her life, *"Sentimental Journey"* and *"Chattanooga Choo Choo."*

The visit by the President provided Mother her first opportunity to entertain political royalty, which did nothing but enhance her growing reputation as an entertainer for the military. She would later perform for Governors, Presidents, and other political dignitaries, but none would compare to this one. Less than one year later, JFK would be assassinated in Dallas.

Our Heart Belongs to Daddy

"Boy, I love Ms. Emma. She is something. Your whole family
is something!"
"Thank you very much. That's nice of you to say."
"You know, this might sound odd, but I don't ever hear anything
about your Daddy. Did you ever have a Daddy?"

Those who did not grow up with the Kelly's, and only knew us through
the lens of Mother's celebrity, often asked that question, and many times,
just as awkwardly. Those who grew up in Statesboro with the Kellys
knew the man his friends called, *George R.* He never knew his own father.
He grew up around large families, but experienced the solitude of being
an only child. He had a tall and lanky build that reminded others of his
childhood hero, Charles Lindbergh.

His childhood friends described him as having a devilish, impish sense
of humor. He knew how to hold his own in a crowd, and he had the
ability to be the center of attention, if he chose to do so, though his
circumstances and his fate, would dictate otherwise.

He owned and operated a sign painting business, called "Signart
Displays", and his shop was located behind what is now the Averitt
Center and Emma Kelly Theater. He painted storefront signs and
office shingles for most all the businesses in town. He painted the signs
on the sides of trucks and commercial vehicles. He painted the large
billboards on the highways up and down the major thoroughfares
around Statesboro. His business was a full-time endeavor keeping him
at his shop six, and many times, seven days a week.

Dad married a liberated woman, long before the term or concept existed. More times than not, it was Dad who oversaw the routine issues of the family. From dinners to household chores to homework to settling the crisis of the day, when Mother was out performing, Dad was home, minding the store.

Dad was a 'roadie', long before *that* term or concept existed. He was the man behind the scenes for many of Mother's productions, especially those that included the kids.

He set up the sound systems. He delivered costumes, and more importantly, on many occasions, he delivered the performers. He knew Mother's music and the business side of her music, because, much of the time, he was the man behind the scenes making it happen. There were two analogies or comparisons that I think most aptly fit Dad's life and role in our family. The first was a comparison to Amelia Earhart (one that Dad, as a pilot, particularly enjoyed).

At the height of her fame, few people knew that Amelia Earhart was married, while in fact, it was her husband that was the brains and the organization behind her flying career. She was the face of the enterprise, but her husband was the support behind the scenes.

That was Dad.

The second comparison was an analogy that a close friend of Mom and Dad's used to describe the two. He said, if the Kellys were a ship, Mother would be the sail. She was the face of the ship that everyone saw as the ship pulled into port. Dad was the rudder and the keel, working out of the public's eye, ensuring that the ship stayed afloat and on course. Dad was that foundation... both to Mother and to us.

The question most often asked of us was, 'Did your parents intend to have such a big family?'

While none of us remember Mother or Dad stating explicitly their intentions to have ten children, there was ample evidence to suggest that they may not have embarked on that plan, but they certainly didn't back away from it.

For Dad, having a house full of children could have taken him back to his own childhood, one in which he grew up amongst a large extended family of cousins, aunts, and uncles, but never knew the joy or the experience of a father or brothers and sisters. Dad's most joyful moments seemed to come when all of the family was around. With the chaos and noise that came with a house full of children, he could sit back quietly and enjoy.

The irony was that Dad had that impish and outgoing personality and sense of humor, and he was fully equipped to hold his on in social settings. In the presence of Mother or his children, however, he was perfectly content to sit back and become part of the audience. He once said, "I could compete with your Mother or with the kids. But why would I want to do that when I can just sit back and take it all in?" That is what he did best and enjoyed most. He took it all in.

As the size, demands and challenges of the family consumed more and more of his time and energy, Dad managed to cling to his one form of self-indulgence... flying.

He loved to tell the stories of developing his love of flying as a youngster, and being hooked when, at the age of fourteen, he followed the flight of Charles Lindbergh across the Atlantic. He told of learning to fly in World War II, where one of his assignments was to fly a mail plane, which, coincidentally, was an early assignment Lindberg had in his career. Given those parallels in their flying careers, combined with the similarities in their tall and lanky physical characteristics, Dad enjoyed the comparisons to 'Lucky Lindy.'

In those rare moments, typically on Sunday afternoons, he found complete peace in the skies at the wheel or stick of a Piper Cub or Cessna. He was as much at home giving flying lessons or serving as Commander of the local Civil Air Patrol Squadron, as he was being a Dad. No matter the many challenges he faced - from a full-time business to run, a liberated woman to accommodate, and ten children to feed, clothe and house - as long as he could steal away for a few hours on a Sunday afternoon to enjoy those moments of peace in the skies, all stayed right in his world.

Dad's values were simple and straightforward…

> *"Do what you say you're going to do."*
> *"Tell the truth."*
> *"Under promise and over deliver."*
> *"Do what's right."*
> *"Look a man (or woman) in the eye when you speak."*

There was nothing confusing about Dad's messages and his expectations.

Between his work, Mother, and the ten of us, he was always expected to be in several places at once. Nevertheless, none of us can remember an occasion in which he wasn't there for us. He was with us every day when we were growing up… and he has been with us every day since.

Hits and Near Misses

Despite our size, show business responsibilities, and the limitations of our finances, we managed to experience all the normal activities that typical families enjoyed in the 1960's. Along the way, we experienced some nice moments, and dodged some pretty serious bullets.

We participated in the 4th of July celebrations at the Recreation Center. We had family reunions at a place on the Ogeechee River called Redbug Haven. We played in Little League games, football games, basketball games, swimming lessons, sock hops, and school proms. We took class trips to Atlanta, Washington, and New York. The girls had Sweet Sixteen Birthday Parties, went to summer camps, performed in theater. We enjoyed opportunities to do just about everything there was to do in the 1960's, and in many cases, we excelled.

Kitty became an accomplished pianist and vocalist. Pat enjoyed her professional dance career in New York. The boys participated in all of the athletic and sporting events at the Recreation Center. Bill and Mike excelled in basketball and football, and both received scholarships to continue sports in college, Bill at Georgia Tech and Mike at Davidson.

We pursued every form of extracurricular activity the town of Statesboro had to offer, and we pursued them with the same appetite we had for music.

We also encountered our share of mishaps…

At the age of seven, Pat was diagnosed with Rheumatic fever, and was confined to bed rest for three months. Trying to remain in bed for an extended period of time in the Kelly household was like trying to remain calm amidst swarming bees. There was simply too much activity and too many demands. Still, Pat persevered and became the woman and mother that she is today.

In the summer of 1963, Paula was attending a wedding in nearby Reidsville. She was riding in the motorcade that followed the bride and groom as they left for their honeymoon which turned into a chase. The car that Paula was riding in lost control and crashed. Mother had played piano at the wedding and was driving back to Statesboro. She was one of the first to come upon the crash site, and was one of the first to discover her daughter badly injured. Paula's pelvis was broken, and the prognosis for a full recovery was not good. The doctors were doubtful that Paula would be able to walk. They also warned that her injuries may have destroyed any chance for her to have children.

The family rallied around Paula throughout her rehabilitation. Through prayer and sheer determination, Paula defied the medical prognosis, and made a full recovery, and became the woman and mother that *she* is today.

Pete experienced epileptic type seizures as a teenager that perplexed Mother and Dad, as well as the doctors. His illness and the confusion he experienced during those times brought him as close to death as any of us. He survived, made a full recovery, and became the man that he is today.

Through every adversity, the fire that destroyed the family home, Pat's illness, Paula's accident, Pete's illness, and all of the other challenges we encountered, we recovered. As the commercial used to say, *we took our lickings, and kept on ticking.*

Moving On

By the mid 1960's, the structure and routine of the family had shifted. Though there were ten children, there were now fewer living at home and the family began to get a glimpse into the Kelly clan would look like as adults.

Kitty became the first of the Kelly's to complete college when she graduated from Georgia Teachers College, and soon after, she became the first to get married and the first to make mother and Dad grandparents. She married Joe Walters, who was stationed at Ft. Stewart as a member of the Army Band, and who moonlighted as a trombonist with mother's dance band. Not long after they were married, they produced the first Kelly grandchild, Laurie Lynn Walters.

The next generation of Kellys had begun.

Kitty and Joe were living in towns like Soperton, Greensboro and Folkston, where Joe served as the high school music director.

As Kitty and Joe began their family and their lives together, the rest of the children were not far behind in the pursuit of their lives, families, and careers.

Phoebe finished college at Georgia Southern, and after living in Tennessee and Florida, moved to New England when she married Bruce Collins.

Jackie had graduated, and was now teaching school in Atlanta.

Paula married Lawrence Rogers, and the two of them settled in nearby Eastman.

I had married Brenda Perry, whom I met while in the Air Force, and returned to Statesboro to finish school at Georgia Southern and then graduate school at the University of Georgia.

Bill won a scholarship to play football at Georgia Tech, where he was recruited and signed by the legendary coach, Bobby Dodd.

Mike, a Rhodes Scholar finalist in high school, received a football scholarship at Davidson College, where he would finish and go on to law school at Vanderbilt University.

At this point, Emaline was now the oldest sister at home. While going to school at Georgia Southern, she assumed the role of managing the Kelly household and had succeeded me as the drummer in Mother's band.

Pete and Pat remained at home finishing high school and were the remaining Kellys in Mother's show business performances.

As always, Dad was right there with them, serving as the foundation and the glue that held everything together.

With most of us now having families of our own and spreading to places like Eastman, Atlanta, and Boston, family gatherings became more logistically challenging, but all the more gratifying. With each new wedding, each new in-law, each new baby, the family expanded in numbers and in richness. Holidays, such as Thanksgiving, took on increased meaning and importance, especially for Dad. As the children started families of their own and provided new grandchildren to enjoy, the man who had never known his own father seemed to relish his role as a father and grandfather.

Dad was also now in a position to travel and enjoy the events of his children and grandchildren. He traveled to watch his children perform in musicals, football games, and marathons. He joined them to take trips to Hawaii, Bermuda, San Francisco, and Boston.

Things that he did not have the means or the time to do when the children were growing up, he was now able to do. He loved every minute of it, and he did not want to be left out of anything.

In 1981, the family went on a skiing vacation together in New Hampshire, and if his family was going skiing, so was he. Though he had never been on skis before in his life, he took lessons at the age of 68, and joined us on the slopes as a novice skier.

While many outside the family assumed we got our personality and characteristics from Mother, those close to the family knew that much of the grit, tenacity, and determination that we exhibited came from Dad. Those were all characteristics that we took into our lives as adults and the lives of our own families.

45th Wedding Anniversary

As each of the ten of us became adults with families of our own, we developed a growing appreciation for both who we were and what we had become as a family. As individuals, each of us could be regarded as bright, talented, and outgoing. Together, however, the whole seemed to exceed the sum of the parts.

When we came together as a family, we seemed to feed off of each other, and everything seemed to get magnified. We talked louder, laughed harder, and the bonds got tighter. When the family gathered together, special things seemed to happen. None could compare to our gathering in May of 1982.

In the previous year, several members of the family attended a 50th wedding anniversary celebration in New England. It was a celebration for Phoebe's in-laws, and left all of us thinking about doing something similar for Mother and Dad on their 50th, which would occur in six years.

As we began to discuss the topic with the remaining brothers and sisters and in-laws, my wife Brenda brought to our attention that we might·not want to wait that long. With Dad approaching 70, and Mother not far behind, she suggested we may want to consider doing a 45th anniversary party, and then do it again in five years for their 50th, assuming we had the opportunity. It was an excellent suggestion. One that we fortunately heeded.

We concluded that a 45th Anniversary party would be a good reason to celebrate and could serve as a warm-up for their 50th anniversary. So, the planning began.

The date was set for a weekend in May of 1982. We told Mother and Dad that we wanted to celebrate their anniversary, which would offer a convenient opportunity to get the ten of us and our families together. What we did **not** tell them was that we began contacting all of their brothers, sisters, aunts, uncles, cousins and friends to arrange a much larger surprise celebration.

The event gave Mom and Dad the surprise, and many would say the celebration and memories, of a lifetime. It would turn out to be the most momentous occasion of their marriage, and perhaps the highlight of our family's existence.

After months of planning, the ten of us and our families arrived in Statesboro on Friday afternoon. We began the festivities with an outdoor barbecue at Bill and Laurie's. The afternoon and evening was filled with good food, good drink, lots of reunion time with the brothers and sisters and families, and the usual fiercely competitive basketball game.

The next day was a restful and relaxing Saturday by the hotel pool, in preparation for a motorcade drive down to Savannah, where Mother was performing that night. As was always the case when we were growing up, Mother would not allow her children to be present at one of her shows without having us perform.

In front of an unsuspecting audience, we revived the old song and dance routines we performed as children. Each of the children took turns doing old soft shoe routines. We performed dances we had not performed in twenty years. We sang duets. The sisters performed dance routines together, followed by the four brothers performing a rusty time-step routine.

Brother and sister song and dance routines were delivered to an audience who received much more than they had expected for what they thought would simply be an evening of entertainment with Emma Kelly.

G. Ross Kelly

At the end of the evening, we left the venue for the drive back to Statesboro, all believing Saturday night would be the highlight of the weekend. We were wrong.

Sunday morning, we all went to church together again at the First Baptist Church, just as we had done on so many Sundays as children. We then adjourned to the Forest Heights Country Club for a Kelly family lunch, and it was just as we had planned it. We all enjoyed a private family meal together, almost like a Kelly Thanksgiving gathering, but with someone else doing the cooking and meal preparation.

When lunch was completed, we did family photos, which was always a family requirement, and gave every indication that the weekend was coming to a close. Mother and Dad were both genuinely pleased at what they felt was an extraordinary anniversary weekend celebration.

Then the real fun began.

The dining room where we had lunch was separated from a much larger dining area by a collapsible curtain. Just before we adjourned, we told Mother and Dad we had one more item of business to tend to. We opened the collapsible curtain, revealing more than one hundred of Mother and Dad's friends and family members who had secretly and quietly assembled to join in what would be the REAL celebration.

Mother and Dad were brought to tears. They were both genuinely surprised and overwhelmed that we could have pulled all of this together, without any of it leaking. It was as if taken from the old 1950's television show *"This is Your Life"*.

What began as a somewhat ordinary anniversary celebration turned into a series of personal tributes to Mother and Dad by their children and grandchildren and their lifelong family and friends. The ten brothers and sisters once again performed one of our old standards with a rendition of *"When You're Smiling,"* and what would be a sign of things to come - the next generation of Kelly's got into the act. The grandchildren gave their grandparents their very first performances as part of the Kelly clan.

124

After the entertainment, each of us along with several friends and family members gave tributes to Mom and Dad and our family, sharing touching tributes and remembrances. The laughter flowed, along with the emotions. It was classic Kellys… music, dancing, laughing, partying, and enjoying being with family. Even beyond the stories and the music, perhaps the most moving aspect of the day was the remembrances that each of the ten children shared about what it was like to grow up as a Kelly.

The stories were funny, poignant, and very moving, and the afternoon was an emotionally drenched combination of laughter and tears. No one who was there, family or friend, was untouched by this very special occasion. Each of the ten of us spoke, and each of us had difficulty holding back our emotions as we shared our experiences and memories as member of the Kelly family.

At the end of the gathering, one of Mother and Dad's closest friends, Robert Zetterower, seemed to sum up the day in his own tearful tribute.

> *"I've been around this family a long time. And we've had George and Emma and every one of these children at our house on many occasions. And I have never known a family with such love as there is in this room today. George and Emma, you are two very lucky people."*

Mother, the consummate entertainer, could not speak, and when we offered the microphone to Dad, who was also never at a loss for words, he simply buried his eyes in his handkerchief, and waved us off.

We pulled it off. We had managed to pull together every one of Mother and Dad's family members and close friends to give them their recognition. *And* we had each managed to say to both of them what had been in our hearts for many years, but had not spoken. We managed to give them the anniversary celebration of a lifetime.

To top it all off, we had managed to render both of them speechless. Though Dad could not corral his emotions to express his thoughts on that day, he did write each of us a letter a few days later, to share his reflections on the occasion.

> *Handwritten letter from George Kelly, following the Wedding Anniversary Party (You must imagine a number of smiley face icons and LOL's to appreciate his humor throughout the letter)…*
>
> *"Despite my desire to follow very closely the precedent established by all my sons and daughters, I blew my chances of wowing each of you as an after dinner speaker this past Sunday, by letting my heart get into my throat.*
>
> *So I had to find a way to get into the act.*
>
> *I can hear Phoebe groan and end Emaline telling me to get new material, or a new audience, but I was given the 'all clear' by the 'Big Em' to write this. (She still cannot express her thoughts, so this gives me the chance to get a word in. Isn't that a switch).*
>
> *First, I want to thank each one of you for making this weekend one of the happiest ever for Emma and me. To say we were surprised is ridiculous. Stunned, shocked, overwhelmed, overjoyed, thrilled and delighted may partially describe it.*
>
> *I apologize for being pushy, and maybe you still don't know it, but I am the head man. Again, look at all the pleasure of just anticipating all these months.*
>
> *The logistics of the affair were terrific. Now I know how the Pentagon feels when they move a battalion.*
>
> *Aunt Elise. Carolyn Blitch. Aunt Lil and Jackie. Betty and Buck. Bob and Ethyl. Brook and Liz. Paul and Pat. Robert and Jewell. We were all flattered and honored by your presence. But you are certainly getting careless with your reputations. Suppose the word of this riot got out.*

The memories of these forty-five years are most pleasant and filled with much happiness and joy. During those years, Emma would visit home occasionally. And I must admit that most of the time spent with me was either loading or unloading the car.

On that note, a major milestone was reached today when Ross agreed to take the drums to Boston. Hooray!

I used to think Emma was all mine. But one day I saw her picture in the newspaper with the words underneath,

"EMMA KELLY
Savannah's Own."

She sure fooled me.

I never could understand how she could be away so much from such a mild mannered, good looking husband. She must have been influenced by those ignorant people who still are not convinced about my good looks. There certainly are a lot of ignorant people.

I hope she visits home more frequently and decides to stay longer. The first questions she asks when she gets home is, "Where is the mail?' And, "Did you feed the cats?" The cats were always number one, and hopefully, I came in second. (You thought I was going to say, 'Number 2' didn't you. I'm no dummy!)

Bob Bradley introduced Emma and me. As I remember, we had no way to get over from the metropolis of Statesboro to Leefield, except to commandeer the old gray mule and wagon. It was not bad for emergency travel, especially if you take the scenic route. We finally arrived and found Ms. Emma at the family store. One of my favorite departments in the establishment was Mr. Will's wine storage. He used to ask me to taste his wares. He stocked quite an assortment (all his own brew), and before long, they all tasted, "putty dood."

Emma came up to all expectations. Boy, I can still remember that dress! She had more moves than a Falcon quarterback. I still don't think it took all those wiggles just to walk. Little did I know that this was the start of a regular job.

Kitty was the first to arrive. It took two days and nights for her to make her debut. Stubborn from the very beginning. But nice. Smart too. She was picking out tunes on the piano before she could walk. Joe was also a musician. But the way it was told to me, as a musician, he made a pretty good engineer.

Phoebe was the second to arrive. She looked like her daddy then. She excelled in dance. Even better than Bill. She was also the first to make a Yankee surrender. Good work, Phoebe.

Jackie, number three, was next. She came on an afternoon. They didn't notify me of the stork delivery. It was becoming routine. Doctor Floyd told me as he was returning to his office. Soon, Jackie was reorganizing things and straightening us all up. As time went by, she shot down the second Yankee. Yes, the south is going to rise again.

When you were toasting us during the party, Jim said, "I'll drink to that." He would drink to anything.

Paula arrived during dancing school. Somewhere along the way, she acquired all her sweetness and charm. She has done many good things for many people. And occasionally, she does one for herself. Not the least of which was when Lawrence got tired of running, and finally gave in.

The first year in college was a snap for Ross, as he did not let classes interfere with his education. Then the Air Force. Then another Yankee. Though I don't think Brenda thought she had been conquered. Ross, just look at him. Cool, suave, always in charge. That is, until Brenda speaks. Then everyone listens. Ross, remember the time you jumped off the roof with a towel around your head, loudly proclaiming that you were a 'souvenir.'?

Then came Wild Bill. When Bill was small, he had the nicest blonde curls. I think there must have been some confusion as to his gender. He was always taking his clothes off. One day, a very large trailer rig pulled up in front of the house on (Highway) 301. And the driver brought Bill to the door, completely minus any clothes.

Then Emaline makes the scene. She was always my favorite girl, named Emaline. She was so shy, we always had trouble getting her to open up and talk. Later, SHE hooked another Yankee... Big Rock, the biggest of them all. Thanks Em, for not throwing him back.

Mike was the 3ʳᵈ male, and according to him, we had finally perfected the mold. I thought we had done pretty well from the get-go. And we did practice a lot. He was always disgustingly smart. He had all those beautiful girls, and still manages to stay out front. He recently achieved the ultimate goal. He is the proud owner of a Ford pick-up.

Pete patterned his college career after Ross. He has spent most of his adult life at Georgia Southern. But all good things must come to an end. This quarter should finally do it. Pete gave us all the worst scares of our lives. But thank God, we are all still together. I hope someone will help him find a girl. I think he only has three at this time.

Pat is the last of the litter. And Pat rates a 10. Now that's pretty good, isn't it? They say (at least Paula and Pat do) that the best things come in small packages. Having a beach apartment and a Volvo can't be all bad, can it?

We are very proud of our children and their families, and we think you are the best in the world. Though our bank account may not reflect it, we have riches untold.

Thank you all very much. And I thank God for the Kelly's.

Mom and Dad"

At no time in our lives together did we appreciate and understand the true uniqueness of our family more clearly than on that day. Perhaps in a way that we had never realized before, each of us, along with our spouses, in-laws, children, and extended families, discovered that what we had was very special indeed.

Brenda's idea that we celebrate Mom and Dad's 45th wedding anniversary and not wait for their 50th was fortuitous. We would lose Dad two years later.

Forever Thankful

Thanksgivings were the most important time of the year for the Kellys. That is the one time that everyone stopped what they were doing, wherever they were doing it, and came together as a family.

When all of us lived at home, Thanksgivings were important, but they were almost taken for granted. It was when we grew older, got married, and began to spread out, that we began to truly appreciate the importance that it represented to our family. It was then that our family Thanksgiving tradition began in earnest.

Our first official Kelly Thanksgiving occurred in 1960 in Soperton, Georgia. Kitty and Joe moved to Soperton when Joe took a job there as the Band Director for the local school system. Settled into their new home, they wanted to host Thanksgiving to give the rest of the family a chance to see their new digs. With a total of sixteen participants, it was enjoyable, relatively low key, without incident, and was the smallest Thanksgiving gathering we would ever know. From those humble beginnings, the Kelly Thanksgiving tradition had begun.

Each subsequent Thanksgiving, as more Kellys graduated from college, moved away, got married, and began lives and families of their own, the event expanded in size and number, as did the logistical challenges of bringing everyone together.

Sometime in the 1970's, we began the tradition of rotating the event each year, with each of the older siblings taking their turn at hosting the annual gathering. Wherever there was a Kelly, be it Statesboro, Atlanta, Dublin, Eastman, Charlotte, Savannah or Jacksonville, a Kelly

Thanksgiving gathering was hosted there at one time or another, and in the aftermath, the host was left to explain to his or her neighbors what had just happened in their neighborhood.

Notwithstanding the logistical challenges, each Thanksgiving was a joyous celebration, filled with music, football games, basketball games, and just reconnecting. Thanksgivings were our way of getting reengaged with one another, reflecting, and giving thanks. As we became more engaged with our own families, we became even more appreciative of the blessings and good fortunes we enjoyed; we truly embraced the spirit of the holiday to give thanks for those blessings.

Some were more memorable than others, and all had their minor mishaps and glitches.

In 1975, Brenda and I hosted Thanksgiving in Dublin where we were living at the time. At this time, Phoebe and Bruce, Emaline and Rock, and their families were living in Boston, and were flying in for the gathering. As Jackie, Brenda and others were organizing the food and other logistical matters, Phoebe (living in Boston) told Jackie, "I'll take care of the turkey."

Now, Phoebe's message was, 'Bruce and I will *pay* for the turkey." Jackie's interpretation of Phoebe's message was that Phoebe and Bruce would *bring* the turkey. So, the planning proceeded, assuming that Phoebe and Bruce would be bringing the turkey.

When Phoebe and Bruce arrived from Boston on Thanksgiving morning, surprising to everyone, they did not have a turkey with them. We were about to have a Thanksgiving gathering for more than forty people in about one hour, with no turkey.

The chaos and scrambling began.

Swallowing our pride, we checked with all of our neighbors to see if, by chance, they had an extra turkey (or two). Though none of them did, they all offered to share their turkeys. We politely declined their offers. Instead, we found our way to the local Kentucky Fried Chicken outlet, which fortunately was open on Thanksgiving morning. We bought every piece of chicken they had, cooked or uncooked, frozen or unfrozen. This turned out to be the classic win-win. We had our turkey substitute, and the employees of Kentucky Fried Chicken got to close up early and have their Thanksgivings at home.

In later years, Phoebe, Emaline, and I and our families all lived in the Boston area, all less than thirty minutes apart. For us, the logistics and challenges of being with the family were even greater. On those occasions when we could not get down to Georgia for the Thanksgiving gathering there, Phoebe and Bruce hosted the New England contingent of the Kellys for what would be *'Thanksgiving North'*, and we would connect with the larger gathering by phone.

One year, in 1982, the New England contingent actually hosted Thanksgiving, and on that one occasion, the Southern contingent of Kellys traveled north to join their New England brothers and sisters for the holiday. For many reasons, that Kelly Thanksgiving gathering would be the most elaborate and memorable of them all.

I'm not sure how we convinced everyone to celebrate the holiday in Boston that year, but somehow, we did. By plane, by car, by hook or by crook the rest of the families made their way to New England, where the family would enjoy a weeklong New England Thanksgiving holiday. The gathering included our usual Thanksgiving festivities, but with an added bonus. Everyone embarked on a 3 day ski outing in the White Mountains of New Hampshire. We rented the largest ski chalet in the area, where we all took residence and embarked on our Thanksgiving mini-ski vacation.

On the first morning, all of the non-skiers (including Dad) took lessons in preparation for their afternoon on the slopes. Having graduated from their lessons, we all headed for the slopes. Miraculously, no one broke anything. But the falls, face plants and mishaps were endless... and priceless!

Kellys were skiing off of the chairlifts into the trees. Kellys having successfully navigated their way down the slope but unable to stop, ski on into the parking lot. Kellys fell down and couldn't get up. Kellys rode to the top of the slope in the chairlifts, and after realizing the vertical challenge, decided to walk, rather than ski, back down. Some ventured to try their luck at speed racing, and some did so unintentionally. As the day's adventures came to an end, we all experienced the warmth and comfort of the ski lodge and time to share our stories and the memories of a lifetime.

Far beyond the unique circumstances of that Thanksgiving in New England in 1982, it would be forever cherished in our minds because it would be the last Thanksgiving we would experience with Dad.

The George and Emma Kelly Families

Goodbye Dad

Though we were older and more spread out, Thanksgivings continued to be our one time of the year to bring everyone together.

Thanksgiving 1983, it was Mike's turn to host the annual gathering, which was to take place at his home in Atlanta. Everyone was making their travel plans and preparing their dishes and contributions, as we always had; Dad had worked the day before Thanksgiving as he always had. On this occasion, he stayed at the shop a little longer than usual, trying to finish up before he and Mom would travel to Atlanta for the gathering. At the end of his work day, he went home and proceeded to take a shower, where, without warning, he suffered a stroke. He died instantly.

He was 70 years old.

Instead of coming home to celebrate our favorite holiday with our families, we came home to say goodbye to Dad.

The outside world who knew the Kellys, mostly knew us through Mother's notoriety as a musician. Within the family, however, Dad was our anchor, and within an instant, he was gone.

We had endured many hardships and setbacks as a family, but none would affect us like the events of Thanksgiving 1983. Losing him so suddenly and without warning, left us in shock and struggling to figure out how we recover from having lost the very foundation of our existence. We managed to get through the viewing services and the funeral services and all the related activities that accompany the passing of a loved one, but could not seem to get beyond the state of shock from his sudden passing.

Psychologists say that acceptance is the final stage of grief, and we were a long way from that. We struggled to accept the fact that he was gone, and spent the next few weeks and months trying to figure out how to carry on in his absence. With Daddy there, everything in the family seemed to happen naturally. He was the glue. He was always there behind the scenes, as Mother continued her show business career. He was always there with the ten of us as we pursued our own lives and families. He was the cornerstone of the family. He was always a good reason to come home.

There is a time in every child's life when they truly become adults. This was the time for the ten of us. With Dad no longer there, and with mother reeling from the loss of her husband, we had to step in and take responsibility for keeping the family together. Over time, we slowly regained our balance and our resolve. We concluded that the best way to pay tribute to Dad and his memory was to forever maintain the closeness and togetherness of his family, just as he would have wanted. So that's exactly what we did.

One of the cruelest ironies of the life and story of our family is that Dad never got to see the full splendor of the family he was so instrumental in creating. He never got to see the fame and notoriety that Mother enjoyed as *"The Lady of 6,000 Songs."* There was so much that would occur in our lives after Dad passed away, but it was almost as if he knew it would happen all along. Throughout our lives, his most constant refrain when speaking of his family was, *"I'm the richest man in the world."* Maybe he knew all along. Maybe he knew.

Some years following Dad's death, the ten children got together and wrote him a "Dear Dad" letter, to update him on how things were going since his passing. The letter was our way of conveying to him that all he had wished for, but had not seen come to fruition, had indeed occurred, just as he would have wanted.

Dear Dad,

On this 29th day of June, 1997, we have come to bring you a good report. Your legacy is thriving. Your grandchildren are as strong, vibrant and individualistic as your own ten kids. They pursue their goals and dreams heartily, and with the same determination that we, the 'Top Ten' inherited from you and Mom. Many of your grandchildren have come of age now, and are hinting that it is time to allow them to have the spotlight. However, when we all get together we still think of ourselves as the kids, so we feel we need to complete our own emotional fulfillment before this next generation takes over. But we do make concessions for weddings and such.

You would love to hear your daughter-in-law, Patti's rendition of "Fever", one of your favorite songs. You always said you loved to see a beautiful woman stand up and sing a song with style and grace, not waving her arms around 'like a bat', but composed and cool. Well your grandson Ryan's new wife would have certainly won your heart and admiration with her torch song.

Dad, some of us feared that once you died, our family would splinter and drift apart without you as our nucleus. The fact is, you are still very much the heartbeat of the Kelly family, and we remain strongly united as your and Mom's 'Top Ten'. Mom continues to energize and inspire us with her music, and has become quite the star. She may have accepted a few questionable gigs in her day, but we think you would have certainly approved of her most recent one, which was with Clint Eastwood.

Dad, we know you have moved on, and we are certain that God is delighted to have such a talent working for Him. One can only imagine the heavenly outdoor advertisements your have created. But your remain alive in our hearts and hope that you are pleased to know that your legacy continues to grow, not only in number, but also in strength of character.

We pray that someday we will be reunited with you Dad, and with Grandmother Phoebe and Pauline, and all who have moved

*on to their heavenly destinies. We vow to work hard to continue
to bring honor to your memory by doing good work, raising good
families, and by loving each other. We miss you terribly.*

Sincerely,
*Kitty, Phoebe, Jackie, Paula, Ross, Bill, Emaline, Mike, Pete
and Pat*

PART 4

Fame Comes Calling

Life Goes On

The recovery from Dad's unexpected passing was long and arduous, but for ourselves and for Mother, we had to find our way back into the routines of continuing our lives. By the mid 1980's, all ten of the children were now adults, and most with families of their own.

In addition to their daughter Laurie, Kitty and Joe now also had a son, Mark, and were living in Florence, SC.

Phoebe and her husband Bruce were living in Boston, and also had two children, Leslie and Greg.

Jackie met and married Jim Hinz, and they lived in Atlanta with their two sons, Cameron and Corey.

Paula and Lawrence were still living in Eastman, with their three children, Kelly, Ken, and Julie.

Brenda and I were living in Boston, with our three children, Brett, Rob, and Erin.

Bill married Laurie Duncan, whom he met at Georgia Southern. They remained in Statesboro with their two children, Ryan and Brooke.

Emaline had also moved to Boston when she married Rock Perdoni. They had three children at the time, Emily, Katie and Matthew, and would have a fourth Abbey, soon after.

Mike would be the next to marry when he wed Margo Pallardy, whom he had met while working as a lawyer. They would become the parents of three children, Lee, Michael, and Gail.

Pete and Pat, both in their 20's, had not yet married, but would soon marry and have families of their own.

Pete would marry Elizabeth Sullivan and have three boys, Parker, Reid, and Cole.

Pat would marry David Alley, and their family would include Jackson, Sunny, Emma, and Phoebe.

Our individual families grew and spread out to places far beyond Statesboro, but our hearts and our roots remained there, as did the presence and memories of Daddy. Though our individual families and careers were now the primary focus of each of our lives, we seemed to always find ways to balance the demands of their own families with the magnetic pull of our brothers and sisters. It certainly helped that the Kelly in-laws enjoyed - or, some would say, gracefully endured - the family gatherings as much as the children did.

When the family came together, the Kelly children and the Kelly in-laws all blended together. In the crowd and in the mayhem, it was hard to distinguish who was an original Kelly, and who had married into the family. Thanksgiving continued to be the highlight event of each year, along with weddings and other family events that brought everyone together. During the lulls when nothing was planned, we would organize family vacations or reunions just to create an excuse to bring everyone together. Through it all, the entertainment train kept on moving.

Whether on stage or in our living rooms, the Kellys kept singing and dancing as the family kept growing, and Mother was on the precipice of becoming a national celebrity... and a great grandmother.

Here's Johnny!

As we continued to develop our own families and careers, Mother, in some respects, was redefining hers. Perhaps to fill the void after Dad's death, she began to work virtually non-stop.

Earlier in her career, Mother played for dances and shows with her small combo, but with Dad gone and her children grown and on their own, she began to perform more and more as a solo artist. Given the expanded number of venues, she found herself also performing more in Savannah where there was more of a market for a solo pianist. It was there that she developed a close friendship with the legendary songwriter and Savannah native, Johnny Mercer.

It could be argued that Johnny Mercer was greatest American songwriter of the 20th century. He was most known for his classic, *"Moon River"* and other hits, such as *"Fools Rush In"*, *"Laura"*, *"I Remember You,"* *"Come Rain or Come Shine,"* and many others. In fact, Johnny Mercer wrote more than 1,400 songs, one hundred of which were featured in motion pictures. He won four Oscars for Best Song, and was nominated 18 times. He also wrote 23 theatrical productions, including *"St. Louis Woman"* and *"Lil Abner."*

In addition to his career as a prolific songwriter, he also co-founded and was President of Capitol Records, where he worked with artists including Nat King Cole, Margaret Whiting, Jo Stafford, Peggy Lee, and Frank Sinatra.

In short, Johnny Mercer was a giant in the music industry. His career took him to Los Angeles where he spent most of his time, but he always loved coming home to Savannah.

That's where Mother came in. She not only grew up close to Johnny's Savannah home, but she was the ultimate Johnny Mercer junkie. She knew every song Johnny had ever written (she pretty much knew every song that *ANYONE* had ever written), and when Johnny discovered her love for his music, and her encyclopedic memory, they formed an instant musical love affair. You could say that Johnny Mercer discovered Emma Kelly and was instrumental in transforming her from a local musician to a regional and national celebrity. He was astounded by her prolific talents and musical knowledge, and he began to chronicle just how many songs she knew and could play. It was that exercise that led him to dub her, *'The Lady of 6,000 Songs'*, a nickname that would carry her to new heights as an entertainer.

Johnny was living in Los Angeles, but on every trip he made home to Savannah, he and Mother would get together to share in their love of music. He would come to wherever Mother was performing at the time, be it a bowling alley, Holiday Inn, or a supper club in town. There were many occasions when the crowd Mother was performing for, got the surprise of their lives when Johnny Mercer showed up. He sat with her at the piano, tossed out various tunes, and many times sang duets with her as the astonished crowd looked on.

Mother credits Johnny for encouraging her to sing. Like Johnny, Mother never thought she had a 'classic' singer's voice, but using himself as an example, he convinced her that her audiences weren't judging her on her singing voice… they were judging her as an entertainer. He taught her how to 'fake' the high notes that her voice could not naturally hit and encouraged her to think of herself not just as a piano player, but a vocalist and entertainer.

She heeded his advice. It was through her relationship and collaboration with Johnny, and through his encouragement, that Mother began to sing more in her performances. It was also at his encouragement that she produced her first album.

155

Mother and Johnny and Johnny's wife, Ginger, became close friends. The couple insisted that she stay with them at their 'Moon River' house on Burnside Island when they were in town, and on multiple occasions they invited her to their home in Los Angeles. Johnny was convinced Mother could be a star and wanted to give her exposure to west coast entertainment scene. Mother always enjoyed going, but she was just as eager to get back home. She enjoyed entertaining and meeting entertainment celebrities, her heart, however, remained with her friends and more intimate audiences in and around Statesboro and Savannah. Though she may have had the talent to be a star, she did not have the aspirations. Given the choice of performing before a large audience in a major club or concert hall, or in someone's living room, she always chose the latter.

Johnny Mercer was without question the single largest influence in Mother's musical career. The moniker he gave her, *"The Lady of 6,000 Songs"* would become her calling card as an entertainer and would remain with her for the rest of her life.

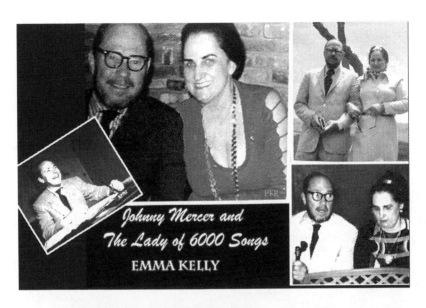

Johnny Mercer and
The Lady of 6000 Songs
EMMA KELLY

Savannah claimed her
Johnny Mercer named her.
Emma Kelly.
"The Lady of 6000 Songs"

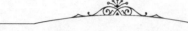

Emma's Celebrity Grows

Seemingly overnight, Mother cultivated a loyal and growing fan base. Her association with Johnny Mercer, combined with her personal charm and talent, made her one of the strongest draws in and around Savannah. Clubs and restaurants in the area began to discover her drawing power, and they all competed for her services and to have the sign at their front door saying,

> *"Tonight featuring*
> *Savannah's own Emma Kelly,*
> *The Lady of 6,000 Songs."*

That was until 1986, when at the encouragement of several friends and investors, she opened her own club on the historic Savannah riverfront. The Lady of 6,000 Songs now had her own venue to entertain her growing fan base. The club was appropriately named *"Emma's."*

Next to Mercer, Emma Kelly had become the most popular entertainer in the Savannah area. And everyone in town wanted to be associated with her. Her fans followed her with a loyalty unknown to most entertainers. Politicians wanted to be photographed with her and celebrities wanted to meet her when they came to town. She met and became good friends and a favorite with the popular Atlanta Journal columnist and comedian, Lewis Grizzard. She became the featured entertainer for government organizations and corporations, performing at conventions and conferences around the state and beyond. She performed for Governors and other state, local, and national politicians.

"Emma's" was not only a fun and convenient place to entertain politicians and celebrities; it was also a fun and convenient place to catch up with family and friends. Anytime anyone from Statesboro went to Savannah for dinner, they would stop by her club for some music and a nightcap, and to say hello. She loved seeing old friends, and they loved the feeling of knowing someone that was now a celebrity.

Men could always count on being able to impress their date by taking them to Emma's and introduce them to Mother. She would dote on the man, tell his date how wonderful the man was, and play their favorite song, whatever it may be. My son Rob told the story of taking a date to see Mother, and while there, heard a man ask Mother, in the form of a quiz to impress his date, "Do you know the Indiana University fight song?" Without hesitation, Mother played the song. He was stunned and his date was impressed. That was just what Mother did, and though it wasn't in business long, *Emma's* was just the place for her to do it.

Though she continued and would always call Statesboro her home, her growing celebrity demanded that she spend more of her time in Savannah. She spent three, four, and sometimes five nights a week in the city, and with the help of friends she eventually set up an apartment in Savannah to minimize her nightly commute back and forth to Statesboro. Despite the convenience of having the apartment in Savannah, however, more often than not, Mother would still drive home after a performance. It was where she was most comfortable, and also where her beloved cats were waiting for her. Statesboro was only a 45 minute drive from Savannah, but most of Mother's drives took place at two and three o'clock in the morning.

In addition to her growing celebrity as a musician, she was also becoming famous with the Georgia State Patrol. She never knew the speed limit on I-16 applied to her, and she was stopped so often that she was on a first name basis with most of the troopers who monitored the stretch between Savannah and Statesboro. Since those troopers' superiors knew Mother well from having attended events where she had played, they eventually instructed their officers not to ticket her, but to simply ensure that she made it home safely. On those occasions when she was not speeding, they would often find her on the side of the highway taking a quick cat nap before finishing her commute home. There were many nights she received a personal police escort home.

Mother's celebrity was on a fast track, but nothing compared to what was to come.

In New York. . .
    it's the Cafe Carlyle

In New Orleans. . .
    it's Pat O'Brien's

In Savannah. . .
    it's
EMMA'S

The Book

By the early 1990's, Mother was performing mostly as a solo artist, and most of her activity had shifted from Ft. Stewart and Statesboro to Savannah. She had gained a strong following in the area, and it only grew with her own club, "Emma's" and her performances at The Pirate's House.

In the spring of 1993, Mother took a break from performing to come to Boston to visit with the New England contingent of her growing family. On this particular trip, she brought with her a manuscript of a book that she said was being published about Savannah, with a chapter in the book, being dedicated to her.

John Berendt was the editor of New York magazine. Over a period of years, he had fallen in love with Savannah after several visits, and decided to write a book about the city and its characters. As he began to scour the city searching out personalities that would form the basis of his book, he was continually encouraged to meet and get to know "Ms. Emma." After an evening of listening to her play and sing, Berendt, like most everyone else who met the woman, was hooked. *"The Lady of 6,000 Songs"* was about to become a national celebrity.

I enjoyed reading the manuscript, especially the chapter devoted to Mother. Having grown up in the area, I found the other chapters of the book interesting as well, including the references to Joe Odom and Jim Williams, whom I had known, and the salacious murder trial of Williams, who was a friend of Mother's and a well-known antiques dealer in the city. The read was enjoyable and the chapter devoted to Mother was flattering, but I failed to see the commercial value of the book. In short, as a book critic, I completely missed what would later become one of the all-time best sellers on the New York Times Book list.

"Midnight in the Garden of Good and Evil" became an international best seller. It remained on the NY Times Best Seller list for over four years, and Savannah, Georgia, the quaint southern city of 17th century architecture and 19th century antebellum attitudes, became a national tourist destination as a result.

As the popularity of the book and Savannah grew, so did Mother's. She was performing regularly at The Pirate's House, and it seemed that everyone who visited Savannah had to check-off all of the spots or the personalities highlighted in the book. *"The Lady of 6,000 Songs"* was one of those items to be checked off. Many of the tourists who came to watch Mother perform, however, had no idea what they were in for. What they expected was an engaging piano player who would entertain them with a sampling of the 6,000 songs for which she had become famous. What they were not prepared for was that they would be pulled into the web of her seductive charms as an entertainer.

As anyone from Statesboro or South Georgia who had seen

Mother play could tell you, between songs, she made it a habit of calling people up to the piano. If they were existing friends, that would serve as her opportunity to catch up on their kids, grandkids, and other aspects of their lives. If she did not know them, she would learn who they were, where they were from, and then ask them that seemingly innocent, but captivating question:

'What is your favorite song?'

Anyone who met Mother for the first time, and told her their favorite song, left that evening feeling like they had a new best friend for life. And they did. More than her encyclopedic memory of every song ever written, and more than her ability to play any song by ear that she heard for the first time, it was that simple question that was the real secret to whatever success or fame Mother enjoyed. It was that question, and what Mother did in response to that question, that gave her instant access into that person's fondest memories and deepest emotions. Whether it was the birth of a child, the first date with their husband or wife, or a memory of their father or mother, their favorite song had something to do with a very meaningful time in their life.

When Mother played their favorite song, an instant bond was formed with anyone who ever sat on the piano bench next to her.

It is fair to say that "the book," as it came to be referred to in and around Savannah, was a game changer, both for Savannah and for Mother. Almost overnight, she was featured on *Good Morning America*, *The Today Show*, the A&E Network, and all variations of local media that followed and documented the resounding success of *"Midnight."* Savannah was now an international tourist attraction, and Mother, along with Lady Chablis, and other characters featured in the book, was a must-see for anyone visiting Savannah. Her engaging personality only cemented her status, not only as a very talented musician, but the personification of 'southern charm.'

Mother was in more demand than ever, and despite her age, she was determined to accommodate any and every request. As she was so famous for saying, *'when people ask you to play, you play.'*

In addition to her nightly performances at The Pirate's House, she soon found herself on a national book tour, which included readings from the book by Berendt, intertwined with musical performances by various artists. In addition to Mother, the tour included fellow *"Midnight"* character, "The Lady Chablis," and other performers including Bobby Short, Gerry Mulligan, Margaret Whiting, John Pizzarelli, and others. Mother and her fellow performers traveled to New York, Washington, the West Coast, and other cities in between.

One of the concerts was conducted at the famed Avery Fisher Hall at the Lincoln Center in New York, and provided the family yet another opportunity to come together and celebrate Mother's late life success. All ten of the brothers and sisters and various family members converged on New York City for the star studded show, and they enjoyed the performances and the mingling with fellow musicians and recording artists backstage and at parties associated with the event. Mother performed flawlessly and felt right at home with her family and her fellow performers. Her fame was quickly expanding far beyond Savannah. She was now cultivating new fans from coast-to-coast. The book was a transcendent time in Mother's career and life, but that was only half of the story. Enter Clint Eastwood and the movie.

Clint Eastwood, the actor turned director, purchased the movie rights to "*Midnight*," and in 1995, he and his crew converged on the city to begin filming the movie version of the popular book.

The Hollywood legend, most known for his tough guy roles as "Dirty Harry," had transformed himself from an iconic actor to an accomplished film director. He assembled an impressive cast for his movie, including Kevin Spacey, John Cusack and Jude Law, and also planned to include several of the characters from the book.

Eastwood, a talented musician in addition to his talents as an actor and director, quickly discovered that he and The Lady of 6,000 Songs possessed a shared passion for music. Though she was not originally slated to be in the movie, Clint made the mistake of spending time with Mother, during the filming of the movie, listening to her play his favorite songs. He sat on the piano bench next to Mother while she played, and the more he listened and sang along with her, the more he became convinced that she should be in the movie. In no time, he had modified the script to work her into the movie.

Having only recently gained celebrity status from the book, Mother was now being given a cameo role in the movie. Her appearance took place in the scene in which Jim Williams was hosting his infamous annual Christmas party. This was familiar territory for Mother, as she had been a close friend of Jim Williams for many years and had performed for many of his parties, in the exact scenario as she portrayed in the movie.

Mother thoroughly enjoyed the experience of being a part of the movie, and getting to meet the members of the cast, but nothing paralleled her enjoyment of spending time with Clint Eastwood, and not necessarily for the reasons one might think.

Clint and other members of the cast and crew enjoyed relaxing with Mother at the piano, taking turns having her play their favorite songs, but she was almost indifferent to them being celebrities. She was less interested in their star status, and more interested in their love of music. Her enjoyment in spending time with the likes of Clint Eastwood, Kevin Spacey, John Cusack and others from the cast and crew of the movie was not rubbing elbows with Hollywood stars; it was engaging those Hollywood stars in her music.

Be they Hollywood stars, tourists from Michigan or Ohio, or her friends back home in Statesboro, all her audiences were the same, and all her music was about the same thing... their favorite song.

"Midnight in the Garden of Good and Evil," the book, the movie, and all of the ancillary media and publicity and attention derived from the total experience, catapulted Mother into a level of fame and notoriety that she, nor any of us could have ever predicted.

Through it all, she never changed. Not one iota!

With the growing popularity of the book and the movie, Mother gained more opportunities to perform in larger, more commercial venues like New York, Las Vegas, or other places that could be characterized as 'the big time.' To the disappointment of those who may have had a purely commercial interest in Mother's career, however, she would, on more occasions than not, choose to stay close to home and play, instead, for a local anniversary party or birthday party of one of her longtime friends. She was never as comfortable in large venues as she was in the small intimate settings where she could get to know everyone in the room and perform for each one of them, 'their favorite song.'

MIDNIGHT FRIENDS

The Hall of Fame

By the mid 1990's, with the notoriety and fame brought on by the book and the movie, Mother had a musical following numbering in the hundreds of thousands. Many of her fans, however, felt that she did not do enough to promote herself or receive the recognition and stature warranted by her accomplishments.

Within those circles, a number of political and business leaders around the state began to lobby for Mother's induction into the Georgia Music Hall of Fame. Visits were made to the State Capitol; letters were written to Governors and Senators. It was a grass roots marketing campaign that finally paid off.

The Georgia Music Hall of Fame had a distinguished honor roll.

Ray Charles
Brenda Lee
Little Richard
Lena Horne
Ray Stevens
Tommy Roe
Billy Joe Royal
Peabo Bryson
Otis Redding
The Allman Brothers
And more…

On the night of September 19th, 1998, the name of Emma Thompson Kelly would be added to that distinguished list, as the crowning jewel on her late-blooming career.

The induction ceremony took place at the World Congress Center in Atlanta. It was televised across the state and was a grand event, reminiscent of the Oscar's or the Grammy's. The ceremony included several past inductees as performers and was hosted by Country and Western artist, Bill Anderson. I was given the honor of giving Mother's induction speech, and when the time came, I milked it for all the moment would allow. I had a lot to say about Mother and our family, and I squeezed as much as I could into the ten minute time limit that was allotted:

> *"How is it that a woman who*
> *never had a hit record;*
> *never wrote or published a song;*
> *never had a recording contract;*
> *never appeared on American Bandstand, Hit Parade, Shindig,*
> *Hootenanny, Soul Train or MTV;*
> *never had her picture on the cover of the Rolling Stone;*
> *and never even had an agent...can be awarded the highest honor*
> *a musician can receive in the state of Georgia?*
>
> *Every day for the past sixty years, in her hometown of Statesboro,*
> *Emma Kelly played piano for Rotary Clubs, Lions Clubs,*
> *Kiwanis Clubs, school plays, church socials, tap dance recitals,*
> *weddings and anniversary parties.*
>
> *And by night, she played the dance club circuit. Traveling*
> *throughout Georgia, Florida and South Carolina, either by herself*
> *or with her combo, she performed in dance halls, American legions,*
> *VFW's, Moose Lodges, Elks Clubs, country clubs and military*
> *bases. And in the midst of this non-stop musical marathon, she*
> *also, with a great deal of help from her husband, managed to raise*
> *ten children.*

Together, they managed to ensure that each child was college educated and grounded in the principles of Christianity, family, hard work and citizenship.

And not surprisingly, she also managed to ensure that each was musically trained in order to weave them into her performances as musicians, tap dancers or singers.

Emma Kelly, the pianist became Emma Kelly and Family. It seemed that as her family grew, so did her popularity.

She has performed for every Georgia Governor since Marvin Griffin and Ernest Vandiver, up to an including the Honorable Zell Miller, who is with us tonight.

She has performed for Presidents Eisenhower, Kennedy and Carter.

She was a close friend and collaborator of Johnny Mercer, who dubbed her "The Lady of 6000 Songs." He gave her this name, not because she knew every song he had ever written, but because it seemed she knew every song ANYONE had ever written.

She was featured in the New York Times best seller, "Midnight in the Garden of Good and Evil", and at the tender age of seventy-eight, she became a Hollywood starlet, when she portrayed herself in the movie by the same name.

These are wonderful highlights to an extraordinary career, But this is not why she is her tonight.

She is here tonight, not because of how many records, tapes or cd's she has sold, but because of how many lives she has touched.

She is here tonight, because over the past sixty years, she built her audience, which now numbers in the thousands, one individual at a time.

For if you ever heard Emma Kelly play the piano at one time or another, you sat on the piano bench next to her while she played. And she asked you, "What is your favorite song?"

And you told her the song you danced to at your senior prom, or the song you listened to when you and your husband fell in love, or the song you listed to when you brought your first child home from the hospital.

Essentially, you told her the song that reminds of you of the happiest moments in your life. And from that moment on, every time she saw you again, when you walked into the room, without prompting or requesting, she immediately played your song. And whether in a room of 40 people or 400 people, she was performing for only you.

She is here tonight because each of us has a fundamental need as we try to manage the challenges and complexities of our lives, to hold dear to those moments or occasions that brought us joy and meaning. And music, like no other art form, has the extraordinary power to instantly connect us to those moments. And no one performs that magic, like Emma Kelly....."

The shows' producer had thought it a good idea to have the family gather backstage as I gave the speech, and as Mother was introduced, the curtain would open to reveal the entire family.

"What better way to illustrate the special and unique nature of your Mother's accomplishments," he said "than to have fifty plus family members emerge on stage behind her as she is introduced. Man, that's good television!"

As I concluded my introduction, Mike, Bill and Pete escorted Mother to the stage, as the rest of the family and I awaited her arrival onstage. She received a rousing ovation from the packed house of fans that had grown up listening and dancing to her music. She never looked more beautiful and she was never more proud. She wore a brilliant red, sequined gown and absolutely basked in the glory of the evening.

As she arrived onstage, Emcee Bill Anderson escorted her to the piano where she spoke briefly before performing a brief medley of her songs. She, too, was visibly moved by the moment and had difficulty expressing her thoughts, but as always, her music spoke for her as she flowed through her songs.

Emma Kelly had become a genuine star. Well into her seventies, her musical career was reaching a level that no one could have imagined. Featured in a national best-seller and playing herself in a movie produced and directed by Clint Eastwood, the wife and widow of George Kelly, the mother of ten children, the local entertainer who made ends meet playing for local Elks Clubs, Moose Clubs, American Legions, anniversary parties, and dance halls, was living in heady times.

The Hall of Fame induction was one of those magical evenings. The ceremony was not just a celebration of Emma Kelly the entertainer; it was the exclamation point on an extraordinary life and career of not only her, but her entire family and all they represented. As a friend told the family, "If this were a movie, tonight would be the final scene."

All that was missing was Dad, though his presence was strongly felt throughout the evening and the weekend. Like the rest of us, he would have been extremely proud. And like us, he would have laughed and cried as we celebrated the highlight of an extraordinary career, and a life well lived.

Goodbye Mother

After the Hall of Fame induction, Mother was busier than ever. She was invited everywhere, and as throughout her life, she never said no. Her schedule was relentless, her pace frenetic, and her schedule was virtually nonstop, making almost nightly appearances around the country. But Mother was now approaching her 82nd birthday, and her health, marred by diabetes, kidney and liver ailments, had begun to catch up with her.

As Thanksgiving of 2000 approached, her pace had begun to take its toll. She was hospitalized for a series of tests to combat her weakened kidneys and liver and her worsening diabetic condition.

Mother always had an iron will, and at no time was it more evident than those days when her will battled head-to-head with her deteriorating health and the pleas of her doctors.

Paula and her husband Lawrence were hosting Thanksgiving that year, and as we all made our plans to gather in Eastman to enjoy the celebration, so did Mother. Though her doctors strongly advised her remain in bed, she informed them that she had other plans. Needless to say, she was there with us in Eastman.

With thoughts of Thanksgiving some eighteen years earlier when the family gathered to say goodbye to Dad, we gathered for what we all suspected would be our final Thanksgiving with mother.

Despite those thoughts, however, Thanksgiving was Thanksgiving, and the Kellys were the Kellys. The joy of being together as a family, and having this most special moment made it a joyous and memorable, if not bitter-sweet occasion.

Throughout the day, Mother relaxed on a sofa in Paula's living room, amidst all of the chaos and activities that were typical of a Kelly Thanksgiving. It was an opportunity for her to get some much needed rest, and an opportunity for each of us to steal some rare, one-on-one quiet time with our Mother.

None of us ever know when it is our time, but all indications were that Mother's time was near. So, we wanted to take full advantage of the opportunity. In my time with Mother on that day, we had a warm and loving conversation. She was reflective and somewhat philosophical. For me, it was a very meaningful time with her, thinking this may be our last conversation together. But it was clear she had not resigned herself to the idea that she was facing her final days.

Even if we thought Mother's time was near, and even if her doctors thought her time was near, she would have nothing to do with it. Mother absolutely refused to consider the thought. She had places to be, people to see, and performances to play, and despite any evidence to the contrary, she planned tomorrow and the next day as if nothing had changed.

Since the very beginning of her professional career in the 1940's, the holiday season was always the busiest time of year for Mother, and she had no intentions of this upcoming holiday season being any different. Health issues be damned, she continued to receive endless requests to appear and perform around the state and around the country; she fully intended to honor those requests.

Between performances, Mother returned to the hospital to undergo additional tests, treatments, and operations. As the Christmas season came to a close, the musical legend once again came home. This time, it was to spend her final days with her family.

With the holidays concluded, we all returned to our homes, our families and our routines, but given the state of Mother's health, we all stayed closely connected. Those of us that lived in Boston relied heavily on our brothers and sisters that were closer to home to keep us abreast of Mother's condition. Being 1,200 miles away, I will be forever thankful and appreciative for the regular updates they provided, which did not get much better. Mother's condition continued to worsen. The updates that had been provided every 4-5 days were now coming daily.

I was back in Boston, and working as usual, but like all of the siblings, I remained in constant communication knowing that Mother's condition was in a continuing state of decline. Mike, Bill, Paula, and Jackie were closest to the situation, and bore the biggest brunt of keeping everyone informed and up to date.

On the afternoon of January 16th, I was just coming out of a meeting and received a call on my cell phone from Mike.

> *"Ross, this is Mike. I don't know if this is a good time to talk or not, but I wanted to let you know, the doctors think it is imminent. You probably need to get down here as soon as you can."*

> *"What are they saying? 24 hours? 48 hours? What?"*

> *"They are saying she probably won't make it through the night."*

Anyone who has experienced the death of a parent or a family member knows the gravity of that phone call. Even when you have had six months to prepare for it, you are still never prepared.

I awoke the next morning fully expecting to get the news that Mother had passed away during the night, but to my complete surprise, when I spoke with Mike on my way to the airport, he told me she was still holding on.

I had resigned myself to having said my good-bye's to Mother the previous Thanksgiving, and that she would be gone by the time I got to Statesboro, but with Mike's news, I found myself holding out a faint glimmer of hope that I just might get to see her one more time. My flight connections took me from Boston to Atlanta, to Savannah, and then the drive to Statesboro. When I landed in Atlanta, I called Mike and was once again surprised and amazed when I heard him say, *"She is still with us."* I tried to keep my optimism in check, but that faint glimmer of hope continued to grow. I had one more flight from Atlanta to Savannah, and then the final drive to Statesboro. Is it possible?

As it turned out, it was not. Mother passed away while I was on my flight from Atlanta to Savannah. It was the afternoon of January 17th, 2001. She was 82.

Though I was heartbroken that I did not get to see her one more time, there was no time to lament or grieve. When I arrived in Statesboro, I joined my brothers and sisters and the rest of our families to prepare for the funeral services, and the celebration of life that Mother, herself, had organized.

Mother's death was national news and condolences began pouring in from across the country and beyond. We received cards, letters, flowers, telegrams, and emails from friends and strangers alike.

We received letters from people that had met Mother one time when she was performing at the Pirates House, or at her club, "Emma's", in Savannah. All of them wanted to tell their stories of how she touched their lives, despite for many, having met her for only that one occasion when they were passing through or visiting Savannah as tourists.

We received flowers from lifelong friends. The family, the funeral home, and the First Baptist Church were all overwhelmed with the sheer volume of flowers and condolences that came in.

The morning of the service began with a motorcade from the funeral home to the First Baptist Church, where the funeral service was to take place. We were not prepared for the number of well-wishers and mourners who lined the streets of the motorcade to say their goodbyes. When we arrived at the Church, mourners were standing outside with no more room inside, which was already standing room only. A public address system was installed outside to accommodate those who could not be inside for the service. We were both surprised and touched by the number of people that showed up for the funeral.

The tone of the service was cheerful and celebratory. The Pastor spoke in glowing, upbeat terms of Mother's life. Mike delivered a touching passage from scripture. Bill's daughter-in-law, Patti, sang a beautiful hymn. And I had the honor of delivering her eulogy.

All of us were determined to deliver messages that honored our Mother as a woman who enjoyed a long, joyous, and meaningful life well lived, and who was celebrated and well loved by thousands of people around the world. The service was concluded, just as Mother had directed, with a recessional conducted to the tune of *"Sunny Side of the Street."*

Following a private graveside service, the family proceeded to the Forest Heights Country Club, which hosted a joyful celebration in honor of Mother's life. You couldn't help but imagine that she and Dad, now finally reunited, were up there watching and dancing to the music, as the hundreds below sang, drank, and toasted her life.

It was perhaps, the single best party I, or any of my brothers and sisters, ever attended.

The day's events and Mother's life were so simply summarized by one of my lifelong friends. Having celebrated the event with more than his share of cocktails, he approached me, grabbed me in an inebriated embrace, came close enough to give me the full benefit of his alcoholic consumption, and said, *"Ross, Your Mama had one hell of a run."*

Yes she did!

We bid farewell to mother just as she had wanted… as an entertainer, as a loyal friend, and as a proud mother.

The Next Generation

There is a strong probability that the greatest chapters in the story of the life, music, and family of George and Emma Kelly have yet to be told.

They are the chapters being created every day by my children and grandchildren, and the children and grandchildren of my brothers and sisters. The chapters contain stories of musicians, singers, dancers, actors, songwriters, and creators of music and theater, probably more talented than their predecessors. They are stories of doctors, teachers, accountants, truck drivers, pharmacists, housewives, entrepreneurs, and business executives.

But most importantly, they are stories of mothers and fathers who are church leaders, business leaders, and community leaders. They are stories of PTA leaders, City Councilmen and women, and leaders of volunteer organizations.

They are the stories of the next generation of Kellys.

Over a span of more than sixty years, the family that George and Emma Kelly began in 1938, have now grown to over eighty members and counting. The core ingredients that shaped the family in its origins remain solidly in tact… dedication to family, love of music, strong work ethic, and the focus on education and Christianity.

The ten of us have experienced more than our share of good fortune and success in our careers and in our personal lives, and we have a deep appreciation for the many blessings we've enjoyed.

None of those blessings rival the sheer joy of what we are seeing in our children and grandchildren. They possess the same talent, personality, grit, and grace as their predecessors, and they certainly seem capable of carrying on the proud legacy of Mother and Dad and their Top Ten. Yet, they are so much more.

The third and fourth generations of Kellys are smarter, more talented, more determined, and better equipped than their predecessors to exceed any expectations or dreams we may have had for them. In talent, character, and accomplishments, they have already begun to surpass their parents. They are taking their musical and show business talents to new heights. They are masterful as parents and teachers of their children. They are successful as business men and women. They are leaders in their churches, in their schools, and in their communities.

In numbers, the stories of the offspring of George and Emma Kelly are a rich mosaic of accomplishment and character that is unfolding before us and becoming richer and more beautiful every day.

But as the expression goes...

> *"Where much is given, much is required..."*

Much has been given to our children and grandchildren.

They inherited a wonderful legacy, some incredible DNA, and the opportunity to pursue just about anything in life they might choose for themselves. So, what should we expect of them in return?

I will take the liberty of speaking on behalf of my brothers and sisters, to offer our children and grandchildren these simple challenges that I believe satisfy the requirements. Just like the House rules that governed the ten of us, these challenges are in no particular order, but all are important:

Celebrate the lives and legacy of George and Emma Kelly and the family they created.

Very simply, know and remember who George and Emma Kelly were, and make sure your children know who they were. Know the values that were so important to them. Know what they expected of us, and in turn, would expect of you and your children.

Know the challenges they faced, the hardships they overcame, and the perseverance and sacrifice they demonstrated in facing those hardships.

Know Mother's music. More importantly, though, know the real purpose of her music. Know that her music simply served as a vehicle to personally connect to her audience, and touch the lives of her audience in a way that only music can.

Know Dad's character, his personality, and how he managed his very unusual circumstances as a husband and a father. Know the hollow emptiness he experienced in never knowing his own father, and know the sheer joy he experienced in being with his children and grandchildren.

Know that your mother or dad, as a member of the Top Ten, grew up in rather unorthodox and unusual circumstances, and most likely exhibit some rather unusual behaviors as a result. Know, not just their quirky behaviors, but the experiences behind those quirky behaviors. Never stop asking them to tell their story as a member of the Top Ten and what experiences shaped who they are today and, in turn, who they want you to be.

Most of all, celebrate who you are as a result. You are a descendent of a proud and talented family who wrote the book on playing together, praying together, and sticking together... no matter the circumstances, no matter the odds.

Keep the Mosaic together

Keeping this large and ever expanding family together will perhaps be the biggest challenge you will face as a member of this family. It is, however, the most important legacy you will leave to your children.

We know the challenges we faced keeping the ten of us and our families together as we grew larger in number, and further apart. So, we fully appreciate the challenges you face in keeping an even larger extended Kelly family together, as it grows even bigger, and even more spread out.

But do it!

Take care of your own individual families, but keep the Kelly families together and close. Stay connected to your cousins. Visit them. Vacation with them. Share holidays with them. Know what's going on in their lives, and in the lives of their families. Be the first ones to celebrate each other's accomplishments, and the first to comfort each other in times of grief.

Help each other. Every one of you will have times of need, and every one of you will be in a position to help in some way. This is where the real power of this large, crazy family pays its greatest dividends.

Live and abide by the slogan…

"The power of the wolf is in the pack!"

And you come from a wonderful pack!

Keep the music alive

There is enough music DNA in this family to form a large symphony orchestra. If recent history is an indicator, the genes are getting stronger, not weaker.

Every descendent of Emma Kelly has those genes. Your challenge is to find the talent in yourselves and inside each and every one of your children, and milk it to the max. Train it. Encourage it. Reward it. Celebrate it. And remind them where it came from.

Learn an instrument. Write songs. Perform live music. Perform in stage productions. Support the arts. Do something, anything to exercise the glorious DNA that is inside your body.

Do not let it go untapped. In whatever form or medium it may take, find the music that is in you, and in your children, and perform it with everything that is within you.

Now, in the event you are absolutely stumped as to how to do your part to keep the music alive, there is one, very simple, foolproof step you can take. This is something you can do today, with absolutely no musical or theatrical training, and I challenge you and everyone reading this to try this simple experiment....

Go up to someone and ask them, 'What is your favorite song?'
Then sit back and listen while they tell you their life's story.

How Did We Pull This Off?

It has been more than eighty years since the inception of the story that was George and Emma Kelly, and the follow on story of Mother's amazing journey as an entertainer. It has been more than fifty years since Pat's birth and the advent of George and Emma's Top Ten. As we reflect back on it, each of my brothers and sisters and I ask the same question...

How in the world did we pull this off?

How did we survive ten children growing up in the same household with little or no money?

How did we survive a house fire that destroyed what few possessions we owned, and live in a small two bedroom apartment while Dad remodeled a larger house for us to move into?

How were we, as brothers and sisters, able to remain as close as we have been through it all? How did we manage to not only remain in touch with each other, but remain actively engaged in each other's lives and families?

How did Mother and Dad manage their relationship through it all? How did Dad manage being the husband of a liberated woman? And how did they manage a marriage that defied all the norms of southern life and culture in the 1950's and 60's?

If you ask any of the ten of us, you will likely get ten different theories on the answer to those questions, but there are some commonalities that we all agree on that were major contributors.

First and foremost, there is no question the hand of God was firmly on the shoulder of the Kelly family.

We were extremely blessed far beyond anyone's expectations, and possibly beyond what we deserved, but if God's love ever shown down on a family, it shown down on the Kellys. There were many incidents in our lives that, but for a whisper, could have taken a much more tragic turn. There were many, many moments that captured the phrase, '.... *There but for the grace of God.....!'"*

We were guided by and inherited the iron will of two staunchly independent and determined parents.

Mother and Dad both were determined that they and their family not only survive, but succeed as individuals, as spouses, as parents, and as citizens. Every day, we hear their words in our voices. We feel their spirit in our actions, and we feel their strength as we face our challenges. They were role models for what we should be as individuals, but more importantly, what we should be as a family.

Their strength and the strength of their determination continue to bind us together.

We had the love and support of a wonderful community.

Statesboro Georgia was the perfect place at a perfect time for the Kellys. Our friends and neighbors and the community at large were invaluable in their support for us, as individuals and as a family. Whatever the success or good fortune we experienced in our lifetime, much can be attributed to many people in our hometown that looked beyond our many shortcomings, only to love us, support us, and encourage us to be all we could be.

We had a profound love of music and our musical heritage.

Growing up, every one of us, at times, cursed the notion of being part of Mother's musical performances. The Wednesday afternoon dance classes were a constant chore. Few, if any of us would have chosen to play the trumpet, trombone, clarinet, or saxophone, were it not for Mother's insistence. There were many Friday or Saturday nights when we would much rather have been at dances or parties or football games with our friends than performing at Fort Stewart or some club somewhere in front of strangers. There were more occasions than we care to remember when we were called on to do a song and dance routine for audiences that didn't know us or particularly appreciate our routines.

Through all the years and the drudgery of tap dance lessons, music lessons, Friday night performances and everything else that came with being a Kelly, we developed a profound love of music, and in hindsight, an equal appreciation for the experience. Those experiences not only grounded us in our love of music, they grounded us in our love for each other. Those experiences of being *"The Kellys"* served as the foundation of our love for each other and our lifetime commitment to each other.

Even today we hold those experiences dear to our hearts, and we know the positive impact they had on our lives. When Emaline's daughter, Emily was married, she asked that we perform one of our old song and dance routines. Some fifty years after our first group performances, *"The Kellys"* performed probably our 500th rendition of *"Side by Side."* The crowd loved it, and so did we. It took us back to those days, driving around South Georgia together, hoping our car would get us home. It reminded us of our roots, our family heritage, and the legacy we want our children and grandchildren to take forward.

Music and our song and dance routines, more than anything else, were the glue that held us together, and have kept us together, and with God's grace, will continue to keep us together.

Be proud, Mom and Dad. Be proud!

Epilogue

The Kelly Clan Today

In addition to losing Dad in 1983 and Mother in 2001, we have since lost our oldest sister Kitty in 2014, and her husband Joe, who passed away in 2008. But the circle of life continues.

With each loss, we have added grandchildren, great grandchildren, and recently, great great grandchildren.

As of this writing, the extended Kelly family contains 90 brothers, sisters, in-laws, nieces, nephews, cousins, and grandchildren. By the numbers, as of this writing, George and Emma's family tree looks like this:

1. ***Kitty Kelly Walters, and husband Joe Walters***

   - Daughter, Laurie Lynn Walters
     - Son, Sam Walters

   - Son, Mark Kevin Walters

2. ***Phoebe Kelly Collins, and husband Bruce Collins***

   - Daughter, Leslie Collins Crossett, and husband Don Crossett

- o Daughter, Lila Crossett
- o Son, Charlie Crossett

- Son, Gregory Michael Collins

3. ***Jacqueline (Jackie) Kelly Hinz, and husband Jim Hinz***

- Son, Cameron Kelly Hinz, and wife Christina Marie Hinz
  - o Son, Cashton Kelly Hinz
  - o Daughter, Coralyn Reese Hinz

- Son, James (Cory) Hinz, and wife Fallon Patricia Hinz
  - o Daughter, Addison Cassidy Hinz
  - o Daughter, Hadley Marie Hinz

4. ***Paula Kelly Rogers, and husband Lawrence Rogers***

- Daughter, Kelly Rogers Pruitt, and husband Robert Pruitt
  - o Daughter, Madelyn Pruitt
  - o Daughter, Macy Pruitt
  - o Daughter, Juliana Pruitt

- Son, Kenneth Rogers, and wife Wendy Rogers
  - o Son, Kenneth Lawrence Rogers III (Lance)
  - o Son, Landon Rogers
  - o Daughter, Emilianne Rogers

- Daughter, Julie Rogers Parkerson, and husband Don Parkerson
  - o Daughter, Sadie Parkerson
  - o Son, Micah Parkerson

5. ***George (Ross) Kelly Jr, and (former) wife Brenda Kelly***

- Son, Brett Kelly, and wife Patti Borden Kelly
  - o Son, Finnegan Robert Kelly
  - o Daughter, Grace Elizabeth Kelly

- Son, Robert Ross Kelly, and wife Jill Kelly
  - ○ Daughter, Morgan Kelly Baird, and husband Michael Baird
    - ▪ Daughter, Anastasia Baird
    - ▪ Daughter, Addison Baird
  - ○ Daughter, London Germ
  - ○ Daughter, Emerie Germ

- Erin Kelly Knight, and husband Randy Knight
  - ○ Daughter, Isabel Knight
  - ○ Son, Grayson Ross Knight
  - ○ Daughter, Juliet Knight

6. ***William (Bill) Kelly, and wife Laurie Duncan Kelly***

- Son, William Ryan Kelly, and wife Patti Howard Kelly
  - ○ Son, Patrick Alexander Kelly

- Daughter, Brooke Kelly Stone, and husband Denton Stone
  - ○ Daughter, Ella Stone
  - ○ Daughter, Harris Stone

7. ***Emaline Kelly Perdoni, and husband Renso (Rock) Perdoni***

- Daughter, Emily Perdoni Ware, and husband Nic Ware

- Daughter, Katie Perdoni Kane, and husband Brian Kane
  - ○ Gemma Kane
  - ○ Renzo Kane

- Son, Matthew Renso Perdoni

- Daughter, Abigail (Abby) Perdoni Wright, and husband David Wright

8. ***Michael David Kelly, and wife Margo Pallardy Kelly***

   • Lee Kelly O'Connell, and husband John O'Connell

   • Michael David Kelly, Jr.

   • Gail Thompson Kelly

9. ***Peter (Pete) Franklin Kelly, and wife Elizabeth Sullivan Kelly***

   • Parker Kelly

   • Reid Kelly

   • Cole Kelly

10. ***Patricia (Pat) Lucille Kelly Alley, and husband David Alley***

   • Jackson Alley

   • Sonia (Sunny) Alley

   • Emma Lee Alley

   • Phoebe Alley

About the Author

G. Ross Kelly is one of ten children of George and Emma Kelly. Growing up, he performed song and dance routines with his nine brothers and sisters as part of their Mother's musical shows, and played drums in his Mother's band. After retiring from a successful career in the consulting industry, he founded and serves as Managing Director for EmmaSaid Productions (www.emmasaidproductions.com), a non-profit enterprise dedicated to promoting the art of songwriting, and assisting songwriters in the creation, recording and promotion of their original music.